"I'm not saying I'm going to rule the world,
or I'm going to change the world, but I guarantee you that
I will spark the brain that will change the world."

—Tupac Shakur

Praise

"Luke Mehall carries on in the tradition of the beatniks and the likes of Jack Kerouac. It's an all-American story about seeking out the adventure and dharma of the road, the endlessly changing horizon, and then finding yourself not stuck but rooted into a place that was going to just be one stop along a broad highway of adventure. And in that exploration of a place that captured his soul, Luke is forced to reckon with the pain and pleasure of public lands, a political landscape in great flux, and what that means to a dirtbag climber. But when the place where you can get away from it all becomes threatened—you've got to come back into the rest of the big, messed-up world and argue for change.

My only hope is that Luke never stops writing, even though this book is claimed to be the pent and penultimate of his dirtbag series. It's a fitting cap to his other books and should only launch him out more firmly in the next direction, where just like his many first ascents in Indian Creek, this should take him to new and dizzying heights."
—Stacy Bare, *Adventure Not War*

"Luke Mehall is my favorite climbing writer of the last decade."
—Tom Randall, *Wideboyz*

"Luke Mehall is one of the few adventure writers out there who handles the tricky first-person voice as if it were made for him."
—John Long, *The Stonemasters*

"Who's more in tune with the ethos of the dirtbag—and more able to write passionately and honestly about it—than Luke Mehall? I think no one."
—Brendan Leonard, *Semi-Rad*

"Luke Mehall brings the abstract realm of personal transformation back down to Earth."
—Georgie Abel, *Go West Young Woman*

"Mehall could be the Kerouac of his generation."
—George Sibley, *Dragons in Paradise*

The Desert
by Luke Mehall

PUBLISHER   Luke Mehall *climbingzine.com*

COVER PHOTO   Greg Cairns *cairnsfilm.com*
ART DIRECTOR/DESIGNER   Mallory Logan *go-roshambo.com*
CHIEF EDITOR   Lindsey Nelson *exactedits.com*
ART   Rhiannon Williams *rhiannonklee.com*

ISBN: 978-1-64307-463-4
Library of Congress Control Number: 2018914589
CPSIA Code: PRFRE0219A

Printed in Canada

For Amber

Author's Introduction

This book began when I made my first trip to Indian Creek, Utah, in 1999. For nearly two decades now, I've been exploring this place that climbers simply refer to as "The Desert." This book documents that exploration, both internal and external.

As a writer, I've always felt drawn to "The Truth," yet as I look back on my life, I realize I've been guided by myths more than anything—I think most of us are. The myth that led me away from my childhood home of the Midwest was that freedom and happiness could be found on the open road. I can blame Jack Kerouac and Jerry Garcia for that one. Though those two "heroes" ended up being consumed by their demons, I hope somehow they know the seeds they planted ended up saving other lives, those of us, like myself, that, so far, have been able to live with the light.

Mainstream American culture was what led me to the counterculture. In Jerry's words, "It's hard to find adventure in this new, lame America."

If I'm looking for adventure, The Desert always provides, yet it gives much more. As Edward Abbey put it in his introduction to *Desert Solitaire*, "When traces of blood begin to mark your trail you'll see something, maybe."

The myths of the beatnik and hippie counterculture, which so heavily influenced the early American climbers, made more sense to me than the myths that created mainstream American culture. However, living out the dirtbag dream made me realize I'd probably be headed to a place where I might get a little too acquainted with my demons, so I moved closer toward the middle.

The desert is a landscape I've written off many, many times: too dusty, too barren, too unfriendly, too windy, and too harsh. My dreams have evaporated in front of me too many times.

Somehow in leaving, I always want to come back. Like a long and drawn-out love affair that eventually leads to marriage, the desert has a piece of my heart and always will. I dream about it even when I'm in other rock climbing paradises, sometimes wishing I were there instead of where I am, which is crazy.

Don't worry; I'm not dying. Not yet anyway. We all are headed to that same place though, and that certain ending is what calls us to create. Or at least that's part of the motivation for me. There's really nothing to lose by choosing to be creative, to do something different.

In these two decades of believing the myth of the dirtbag climber—

that, like rock 'n' roll, it can save your mortal soul—I've watched climbing grow exponentially. And that growth has certainly found its way to the desert, especially to Indian Creek. Some older climbers really resent that, or at least lament it, and on occasion I do as well. So I must force myself to look at the bigger picture—we're living on a crowded planet, gobbling up resources at an exponential rate, and if you believe those "fake news" scientists, we're on the brink of a climate crisis, and an extinction crisis. And when you think of those things, more people at rock climbing areas right next to a paved highway doesn't seem like such a big deal. The importance is knowing how to interact with this delicate land.

Besides saving my mortal soul, climbing gave me a job. I've had the pleasure to write the stories, the myths, and perhaps even more importantly, as an editor, I've had the honor to help other people tell their stories through my publication, *The Climbing Zine*.

At one point in the history of *The Zine*, I recall being worried about running out of stories, like perhaps someday, they would stop coming in. That worry, like many worries, ended up not coming to fruition. If there's one thing that climbing provides, it is stories, and the potential is absolutely infinite.

And so is the desert, at least in the realm of what one human can grasp. As I write about the desert, I know that I will only see a percentage of its wonders in my lifetime. I also must note that I am no expert, nor do I have a deep history with this land. I also don't want to be no Wild West cracker, thinking that this land is mine because of manifest destiny. If there is any bullshit myth, it is that this land belongs only to the white man.

When Ed Abbey wrote *Desert Solitaire*, he cautioned the reader about getting in their car and heading to the desert expecting to find what he wrote about. In some ways, that could be said about this book; most of the stories I write about here have taken place in the newly created and recently dismantled Bears Ears National Monument.

That said, even though the Trump administration has tried to dismantle these protections, the place is getting more and more popular, and we need to unite as a people to continue to assist with protections, as well as the education process. The Bears Ears Education Center in Bluff, Utah, seems like a good place to start.

To appreciate a landscape is to know it, and to know how to properly interact with it, we all need to consider our impacts. Old manifest destiny myths are coming back, and we the people must fight back with The Truth.

And if I know one place to find the truth it is The Desert.

Chapter 1

There was an energy to that crowbar in my hand. I was walking alone, down from a cliff, the mission was simple, and it was to retrieve that crowbar, a five-pound piece of metal. When I held it in my hand, I felt violent, and I wished I could use it for good.

New routing had turned me into a madman, a man obsessed. I was obsessed with newness, crisp edges, trundling, creative artistic license, cracks that have never seen the touch of a human hand, obsessed with the lines I'd seen that were unclimbed, and I made up my mind that I, or my close friends, had to be the ones to establish them. The crowbar was a useful tool for this endeavor: prying loose rocks off gently, or not so gently.

It wasn't any sort of manifest destiny bullshit—that was actually what I was so angry about then, right at the beginning of the Trump era. Our mission was one of spirit, not extraction. It was just a feeling, a feeling like this was our time and we had to seize it.

These lines were all over the desert, the Colorado Plateau; the closest rock climbing in the United States would ever be to infinite. Of course it wasn't; if we know anything about Mother Earth by now, we know she only has so much to give, and we are taking more than she has to offer. That's the cool thing about unclimbed lines though—they are already there; we simply open them.

And the reality was, nobody seemed to care. We didn't have any competition. No one else, armed with a drill, bolts, brushes, and a crowbar, was around where we were. Still, the first ascensionist knows a paranoia— that even though you discovered something, maybe someone else had as well. It all seemed too good to be true. But, it was, it was true, and it was real.

I reveled in each and every new route, and the smaller the team was, the less the roar of human beings were present, the more the moment seemed to be at hand. And the closer the moment at hand seems in climbing, the more complete and whole it is, as if you're closer to God. It's funny that we have to teach ourselves to be in the moment in this modern world. I just think most of the world is oh so boring most of the time. The sharp end of a rope was where I felt the most in the moment.

I hiked to one new wall we'd been establishing to get the crowbar and planned to hike it up to another later that morning for use on another climb I was working on. I needed some time alone too; I had anger flowing through my veins. Trump had just been elected president. The pendulum of American politics had swung back, off the rails, back into open white supremacy, open misogyny, simple-minded, ignorant thinking—with just a little help from the Russian government to close the deal. The devil won the election, with fewer votes than his opponent. Classic devil.

That five-pound crowbar swung back and forth, and I hiked down. As the desert does, I sank into the recesses of my imagination. I imagined coming across some white trash piece of shit wearing one of those red MAGA hats. A showdown would happen.

The crowbar would be my weapon—as if a crowbar would be worth shit in a cowboy showdown here in the desert. As if any sort of showdown would happen in this desert at this time—it was 2016, not 1916. *As if the poor white trash was my real enemy—he was not—white trash is a by product of American capitalism,* I'd tell myself, in my conversation with myself. *Get a gun if you really want to be a Wild West cowboy. Why don't you get your shit together, man? I thought you were a peace-loving hippie.*

I was approaching camp now. The crowbar swung slowly, back and forth, back and forth, in my calloused hands. I was expecting camp to be empty by now, desperate for another hour of solitude before I rejoined the crew at the wall. It wasn't, and I locked eyes with a tall blond man. It was Quinn, my friend, not exactly a close friend, but a friend, a member of the climbing crew.

"Hey, Luke, how's it going?" he said.

"Good...good, man," I mumbled, not yet fully out of my trance of anger and solitude.

A quiet settled over us. A tumbleweed may have slowly passed by in the light wind.

Ten minutes went by as Quinn set up camp, and I fumbled through my climbing gear and got ready for another hike. Then Quinn came over. "Hey man, is it cool that I'm here? I mean, I know this is your new area…"

"Naw, man," I said, sort of relieved; he'd sensed my internal anguish. "It's cool. I'm just upset about, you know, the election."

I felt a little awkward and ashamed that I didn't make him feel welcome. No climbing area ever belongs to one person, at least not the in American West; it's all public land. After all, this is where we go to get away from it all, for me at least. This was our own personal paradise. With some friends, some food and water, and some climbing gear, I had everything I needed here, and I wanted my friends to feel that way too.

I thought more about this than what I actually said. Soon there was enough silence piled up that I had to utter something, so I just said, "Fuck it, dude; let's go climbing."

And I don't know if I even said that. But I know we did say fuck it, and we went climbing.

Chapter 2

This is the most beautiful place on Earth, but of course, like Cactus Ed Abbey said, every person carries in their heart an image of the ideal place, the right place. This is just the right place for me. But, right now, something is not right, and it's pitch black anyway, no beauty to be seen.

Chad and I have been rolling his little Honda box car all across these desert roads for hours now, searching for his missing dog, yelling, "Sheila… Sheila…Shelia," only to hear the wind replying.

Chad is a war hero; he lost part of his leg in service to our country in Iraq. He's a climber with one full leg, a below-the-knee amputee. He has a celebrity status in the climbing community—especially later on down the road after he climbed El Capitan, and Mount Everest. This was before all of that.

Then, and now, Chad is just another climbing buddy to me. Most of the time, no disrespect, he seems incredibly normal. This moment, in the dark of the night, was normal, to us. Just a couple of guys, in the Middle of Nowhere, Utah, looking for a lost dog.

Sheila may not have even made a full meal for a mountain lion. Surely too small to be asked to join the pack of coyotes we hear but rarely see. I'm not even sure when the last time a mountain lion rolled through these parts. I've lived amongst the mountain lions for years, but I've never seen one. I can only suspect they are out there. The only things more mysterious than the mountain lion are the spirits, the original inhabitants of this land, back when you could grow corn here. Come to think of it though, the spirits seem closer than the lions—why else would we be drawn here over and over again? Why else would something so meaningless as inching up maroon sandstone walls become so meaningful?

I crack another beer. The silence is deafening.

"Sheila," Chad screams, "Sheila…"

He's hard to read, but I can tell he's worried. He probably feels guilty. He clearly loves this little dog. Earlier in the day, we climbed the South Six-Shooter, a desert tower that is the easiest and most popular in Indian Creek. A nub from certain angles and apparently a gun from others. Everything is about perspective and angle here. Compared to most other desert towers, the South Six-Shooter is unimpressive. But that doesn't mean it's not fun. Sheila got lost somewhere between the approach and the descent, and we assumed she'd be waiting for us back at the car, like any smart dog would do. Or, maybe us smart climbers should have done a better job keeping an eye on her?

We gave everyone a ride back to camp and then returned to search. Camp was a good five country miles away, so by the time our search started, it was pitch black. The moon dictates the light at night here in the desert, where cell phones don't work and the television is the campfire.

Lukewarm beer on dirt country roads has long been a favorite pastime. Sure, it may be technically illegal, but there will never be funding to police all the dirt country roads, so I think enjoying this pastime of beer and dirt is an American right. Dirt don't hurt. Benign civil disobedience. This beer wasn't so enjoyable. I was worried about Sheila and how the coyotes might treat her. Surely they don't realize we are trying to live in a just, respectful country here—they are coyotes, and they don't give a fuck about America!

Thus, in our cars, we were trying to see out into the hidden desert world, and that world can never be seen from a metal box. This was all we thought we could do at the time, drive around and yell from a car. So American of us.

Chad wasn't telling war stories, or any stories really. I've heard his main ones. He's a good storyteller, long and drawn out, like Grandpa. A slow draw. He's a Jack Mormon, I guess—don't let me label him. I just knew he grew up Mormon but seems to live by his own rules now and interacts with the heathens, like us climbers.

I've heard the story about how he lost his leg a dozen times by now around the campfire. When forced with the prospect of amputation, he decided to go for it, that he'd rather use a prosthetic than have a useless limb. The decision seemed to pay off for him. He had a climbing leg, a running leg, shit, the guy even had a party leg: a wooden peg leg. One of his legs, I forget which version, even had a flask built into it.

Chad was clearly affected by this, and by war. He drank away his sorrows, but shit, many climbers drank, as much or more than him, and they never went away to war, so who knows. He seemed to have a small tick, barely noticeable. With long hair and a beard, he looked more like an attendee of Woodstock than a veteran of a foreign war. In a culture where weed is more prevalent than tobacco, a cigarette often dangled from his lips.

All I remember was silence in the car and a hope that grew more distant by the minute that we would find Sheila. The crack of another Schlitz broke the silence, as we turn around and head back to camp. *Fuck, man, I don't know if we'll ever see that dog again*, I thought.

The road back out of there can be glorious at times, something about rubber on red dirt that's just magical. But Chad's car barely had the right clearance, as he scraped the underbelly of that little Honda box more than once. *Just don't hit the oil pan*, I thought. It would be messy and a long walk back to camp. But we arrived back, back to the Superbowl, back to the crew, and they read the news of disappointment on our faces: Sheila was still missing.

The next day, Chad went back out searching for Sheila while we searched for cracks to climb. His terrain to search was vast and desolate, a setting of surreal colors, plants, and rocks. If you've never been to Indian Creek, Mars might be a good comparison because no other place on Earth really compares to the Colorado Plateau.

I didn't go with Chad that day, but I know what he saw: towering behind the South Six-Shooter is the North Six-Shooter, which was really packing heat, standing taller and prouder than its Mini Me, a three-hundred-foot-tall pillar, the most singular and impressive of all the sandstone formations in Indian Creek.

That's the obvious formation, the one that will make the magazine cover or the Instapost on Monday. The subtle beauty is harder to see and doesn't really care if you see it or not. It's just surviving in the desert, like everything else.

I'm no scientist, I'm just a fucking poet, but it seems like, from what I hear, the life depends on the cryptobiotic soil, that chunky black layer that lives on the surface and provides nutrients. "Don't bust the crust" is what they say, and so we avoid stepping on that black gold at all costs. The cows, which usually outnumber the humans in these parts, again, like the coyotes, don't give a fuck about America, and they bust the crust all day long. That karma is on you, cows. But, we eat the cows, so I guess all crust busted by cows is crust busted by man as well.

If I could be transported to any time period to see how people lived off the land, I'd like to see this landscape, a thousand or so years ago, as the Ancestral Puebloans saw it. When they could hunt big game, grow corn, and had access to clean water. When they created the rock art, the pictographs and petroglyphs that we still marvel at today. What lives did they lead, and how often did they smile? Were they free, and how did they talk? Were they as enraptured with this landscape as I am, or was it simply home? Just a place to survive?

I don't have the luxury of returning to that time period, so I guess my imagination will have to suffice. And, I think this engagement of imagination is one reason this land is preserved as it is. Well, maybe other land. Until recently, this was just wasteland, Bureau of Land Management land, or Bureau of Livestock and Mining, as they say. Some say the national parks and monuments were "America's greatest idea." I don't know what that means for this land of leftovers, with little protections or regulations.

The ranchers and the miners were here before us. Miners searching for that uranium, to make a buck, so we could blow up the Japanese in World War II. I don't know how much they found in Indian Creek, a wasteland of sandstone, cactuses, and wind. The ranchers seem to have had a better go of it, and long before any modern climber stepped foot on Wingate, the ranchers had set down their roots and made this home.

I'm trying to get an imaginary whiff of sage and juniper here to reminisce a little more. Trying to see the cactus flowers in bloom, when I know, as I'm writing this, they are not currently flowering. Hearing the piercing screech of a falcon, protecting territory, or their young, flying faster than any bird on the planet, damn near two hundred miles an hour. Stepping in cow shit, god dammit. Better than crypto. Don't bust the crust, man. Not a bad mantra. It's not how you leave your mark in this desert anymore; it's how you don't leave your mark.

But I'm not one of these leave no tracers either—that's bullshit, and all those folks drive their SUVs to the hiking trail anyway, leaving the carbon footprint that's oh so hard to see. Our trace is inevitable; to err is human. We are a doomed human race right about now. Still, that doesn't mean we shouldn't try.

For some reason, it all feels right out here. The cell phone is turned off. Red dirt, red rock, and blue sky—a simple formula, to feel simple again. The mind isn't racing with thoughts of presidential decisions, deadlines, or to-dos. The to-do is simple, and it is to be.

Still, I doubt Chad was mesmerized by much of this that day. I bet he just wanted Sheila to come back. To see that little pup come running, scared and excited into his arms. But mile by mile, inch by inch of searching led to nothing. Chad returned to camp that night again, with only a look on his face revealing the results of his searching.

Sunday had arrived, and it was time to go back home, to leave our treasured sanctuary and return to the grind. Chad wasn't giving up on his search for Sheila, but the longer Sheila was gone, the longer we knew that the odds weren't in her favor. We heard the howling of coyotes at night, and we felt the late-November chill in our bones.

I was returning to my gig as a wordsmith in Gunnison, Colorado. Despite my bark as a beatnik and a descendant of Ed Abbey's, I had no bite. My job was in public relations for a liberal arts college. I sat at a desk, in front of a computer, and crafted stories in the manner advised from the higher-ups. The voice of my pen was not my own. The poet and rebel within me had been tamed, waiting for the day when he could be released into the wild again. I'd deferred my version of the American Dream.

The desert had delivered in its promise I'd stored in the recesses of my mind though. I left home feeling tired and depressed, and now five days later, I left the desert renewed. I'd played in the dirt, used my muscles, slept in a tent, and I felt like a new man. As we drove out of there, I would have been on cloud nine, but I thought of that poor little dog, surely dead, meeting an early demise because it got caught up in the world of climbers.

The drive back to Gunny lasted into the night, turning the pleasant cap of the weekend into deer dodging. Monday morning would come too soon. This was the truth. *At least I would be sore and satisfied while I sat at my desk*, I thought.

I showered, ate some pasta, and went to bed. Around midnight, my phone buzzing awoke me. It was a text. It was Chad. Just as he was getting ready to call the search and head home that night, he'd walked back to his car, and what did he see? Sheila had crawled in, after three days and two nights on the loose, safe and sound. That, my friends, is the magic of The Desert.

Chapter 3

The desert is a place of escape for the climber. Shit, it's all escape, at least for me, escaping this mess we call society. I may not live off the land, but I do live *for* it. Something like that. There's a transfer of energy that I can rely on as much as the sun, but of course, we're just getting started here; I'm reaching. My writing guru, George Sibley, recently told me, "What's the point of writing a book if you know how it's going to end?"

I just know at this point I've got the desert in me and thought it would be interesting to see how it comes out—how recalling stories and fond memories could paint a picture. I guess I've also given up in a way. Given up on humanity, on the belief that we just might save ourselves from ourselves. The desert is the perfect place to be in this state of mind, at least for yours truly, and it always brings me back to a centered place in my mind and my heart. We may be fucked, but the desert says this too shall pass.

Like any love affair, it began with flirtation. I was a college student in the Bush years, those post-9/11 days, the end of innocence for a generation. I was already on the path to "dropping out"—society didn't seem to have a place for me, and I'd discovered climbing, so I didn't feel much of a reason to seek out a place. I would simply live in a tent and go climbing forever. Simple enough, right?

Chapter 4

In Gunnison, where I went to college, winter was the true enemy if you wanted to live in a tent and climb. Forty degrees below zero. It happens. And for a person like myself, who can easily fall into depression, winter was no friend of mine.

In the American climbing world, each area is distinctly referred to as its name: Yosemite, The Gunks, The Red River Gorge, Devil's Tower, Smith Rocks, etc. But The Desert is simply too vast to be contained. That said, The Desert, to me, means the Colorado Plateau, a seemingly infinite expanse of red rocks in Colorado and Utah. Land that used to be the sea. Rocks crafted by wind and rain, leaving behind a canvas on which an artist can create their work, or at least that's how it seems if this land is looked at by a climber. A place so extensively vast I won't risk ruining it by romanticizing about. And I'm not trying to write some fucking *Outside* magazine Top Whatever List anyway. I doubt I'll make any converts out of this book—preaching to the choir, absolutely.

Indian Creek gets all the fame. Canyonlands and Arches National Park too, but more from the tourists bound to their vehicles in a relationship that might border on insanity. Those types of people who go on vacation and bring everything from home with them.

I was raised with Midwest comfort, of safety, stability, and predictability. Hardly a man of the West, but this is America; we have the luxury of redefining ourselves, that is, of course if, we have money. Not everyone in America has money.

In college, gas wasn't much more than a dollar a gallon, so we had enough money to get to The Desert. In Gunnison, we were close to the

Colorado part of The Desert, that which surrounds Grand Junction.

My favorite types of public lands have always been the unregulated ones, the ones where you feel like you're in the Wild West, with more cows around than people, more birds than dogs, with sage, and blue skies above. The Desert has all sorts of this type of land, and it also has the more-regulated land. You'd look for BLM land on a map if you wanted the unregulated, rugged, cowboy-type landscape, and you'd look for a national park if you wanted something a little more manicured and paved. There's a whole lot of gray in between and reasons for protection of lands, but we're still in the red here.

Yes, the red was where the first desert flirtations lay. We'd zip out of Gunnison on a cold winter morning, and by the time the coffee was starting to wear off, we would arrive. We'd either go to Escalante Canyon, a band of sandstone that looks like it was dropped off on its way to Indian Creek, or Colorado National Monument, a wild, protected place, with intimidating towers and rock that ranged from soft to solid.

A flash of memories comes rushing toward me at this point: My thirty-foot headfirst fall in the monument; Mark's thirty-foot headfirst fall a year later in Escalante Canyon; rappelling Otto's Route in the monument in the pitch black with Josh, who was late for his house arrest check-in; guiding high school kids up Otto's Route shortly after that. Wondering what it felt like for John Otto to climb his route in 1911, and just how nuts he really was; bailing off what would later become my favorite route in the monument, Medicine Man, because I was scared of the incoming rain, and then the skies became perfectly blue the minute we got to the ground; climbing this thing called Turd Tower, climbed like it was named and covered with bird poop; climbing with "Bob the Cop," an officer of the law that we somehow made acquaintances with, and he encouraged us to trespass the one and only time I climbed with him, then we got a note left on our car by one of the property owners.

I never climbed with "Bob the Cop" again, not only because of that trespassing incident or because he was a cop but also because he didn't offer me the chance to lead when we climbed with him. He assumed he'd lead because I was a youngster and he was the old trad daddy, and I don't remember a lot of things, but for some reason that little gesture stays with me when I think of my beginning days in The Desert.

So I was a punk kid of sorts, twenty-one and fully abiding by the phrase "tune in, turn on, and drop out" from my beatnik/hippie predecessors. It was the dropping out part that led me to escaping to the desert or other climbing places all the time. Time spent in nature felt like the best way to spend time.

I'd just also come off a period of deep depression that almost led me to suicide—this was before climbing and something I've written about in *American Climber*, so I won't dwell on it too much here, but it's worth mentioning. It's also particularly interesting that I nearly killed myself on accident a couple times, right after I decided life was worth living. They were stupid climber mistakes, like that monster fall I took in the monument, and the time I rappelled off the end of my rope in Yosemite. It's important to dwell and reflect on the mistakes one has made as a climber. So many climbers have had near-death experiences, and to be near to death and to escape without injury—twice—was worth thinking about for the rest of my life.

Escalante Canyon seemed to be one of those places that possessed both a positive, life-giving energy and one that also seemed haunted by the past. I'm a skeptic when it comes to ghosts and houses that are haunted, but I've had a couple experiences that I could simply not ignore.

The first was the "Pete" incident. We'd actually spent the day before climbing in the Black Canyon, the most haunted/enlightening climbing area I know of, and ended up in Escalante late at night, setting up camp at some pull off on the side of the road, a party spot disguised as a campsite, complete with a fire ring full of beer-bottle caps, surrounded by broken glass. BLM land kinda camping.

As we threw our sleeping bags down in the dirt, we all made some small talk and then quickly drifted off to the cosmos. But, just as we were doing that, we heard a voice, which appeared to be coming from just below the cliffs, "Pete…Pete…Pete…"

We awoke from our slumber, and now this was the only thing in the world we could focus on. It kept happening. "Pete…Pete…Pete…"

We looked up to the cliffside to see if we could find a headlamp or any sort of light. Nothing. The voice seemed to get softer and softer but was still crying out for Pete. *What do we do in this situation?* we wondered. We thought we should maybe help, but we couldn't identify where this voice was coming from. Then, we started to really get spooked.

We decided at that moment that we should move the site. Sleep would no longer be comfortable here. And maybe we could shine the lights from our car up on the hillside to find this person, this voice?

We packed up the car in a hurry, throwing sleeping bags and pads in recklessly, and fired up the engine. No more cries for Pete, just three dirtbags spooked in the dead of the night. As we drove past the cliffside where the voice was coming from, we saw nothing. We turned off the car engine and listened for voices. Nothing.

We drove several miles up the road, found another redneck-created campsite and again laid down our bags and weary bones, tired enough to sleep in a place that might damn well be haunted.

Thinking about it more now, I have a hard time believing it was something from the supernatural world, but I also don't have proof that it wasn't. I'm not much of a superstitious person, nor do I really believe in religion or ghosts. But there is a certain energy that Escalante seems to have, and perhaps, maybe, just maybe, there was (is) a ghost named Pete, trying to find his way back home, still.

Just a few months later, I found myself back in Escalante Canyon, with vague plans of where to camp. We were climbing at the Cabin Wall, named so because of an old brick cabin constructed into the sandstone at the parking area. The cabin was built by a veteran of the Civil War, a tombstone maker, who somehow found his home in this obscure canyon, far away from any sort of city. Wild West kinda shit.

We decided that night that we would stay in the cabin. And why wouldn't we? It would be warmer than sleeping under the stars. We caught a nice buzz in the cabin and talked about how cool it was. "Next weekend we should come back with a keg," we said. "Think about how many people we could fit in here." Probably about a dozen or so.

We didn't think much about the previous occupant or contemplate what life was like for him. Was he tortured by the memories of war? Was he a happy loner, content to be out West, away from the duties of civilized life? Was he on the run from something/someone? We fell asleep in total darkness; a more pitch-black place to sleep could not be found in the canyon.

All night, no matter where I was in my dreams, I dreamed I was at war. If I was dreaming I was on a street corner, there were men with guns chasing me. If I was at home, in my dream, I would be on the lookout for shooters. I'd never had dreams like this in my life. It was terrifying. And it went on, over and over, all night.

I woke up cold and exhausted. Somehow I'd channeled the energy of Henry Smith or one of the many guests he had, who sketched their names on the wall above, in a similar manner to the more artistic petroglyphs that the Native Americans had left on sandstone walls across the desert. I never set foot in that cabin ever again.

Chapter 5

War What Is It Good For?

I'd graffiti-ed that in sharpie on the back of my car, shortly after 9/11, and George W. and our government started sounding the war drums in Iraq. There was little chance I'd go to war, a much bigger chance that I'd go to the desert.

I wanted a real American life, and more accurately, I wanted a Western American life. In those times, I was immediately, passionately against the war, yet I attended no demonstrations. In Gunnison, we were hours away from any major city. I wrote my little editorials in the college newspaper, which were probably preaching to the choir—again I wasn't making any converts, never been very good at that; I'm better at reinforcing, I think. A college student in Gunny asked me recently if I would recommend climbing to them if they'd never tried it. I answered that recommending climbing was sort of like recommending psychedelic mushrooms. I wouldn't recommend it, but in the same breath, I wouldn't be the same without it. Doors of perception opened.

In America, there are only two types of men: those who have been to war and those who have not. It seems there is always one war for every generation. At the very least, it is every American's obligation to learn about war. World War II seems like the logical place to start, especially for my generation because our grandparents were all directly affected by it. Most of our grandfathers went, and most didn't talk about it. Mine didn't. He received a purple heart after getting wounded by a bullet. According to my grandma, he didn't feel like he deserved it, when many of his fellow soldiers suffered a much worse fate. He was sent back to the States because he was a good typist, and the military needed someone to write discharges. So I guess it's in my blood to write and not fight. Then again, we don't all go to war like we used to. Thankfully I didn't have to fight in no war, and while I know of the atrocities of it, I never felt it.

My love affair with the desert began in the times of the Iraq war, and also the Afghanistan war, one that still unfolds to this day with American involvement, and my activities in the desert largely were self-indulgent, for the betterment of self. Something like that, again, I'm just stretching out here, just warming up; we've got miles to go.

Basically my goal was just not to die on any given day. The deep depression that I had survived made me think about death, a lot. I liked to think that I thought a lot. I did. I thought a lot about death, and not dying, and how since I easily could have died several times in the last couple years, every additional day I could live was a gift.

I took full advantage of the American right to choose my own religion. I was raised Catholic, and I'm grateful for that. My parents were good people who raised me to value friendships and respect my fellow human beings. There was a major blowup when, at nineteen, I declared that I didn't believe in Christianity anymore, but the dust settled like it often does, and it was never a major barrier in our relationship.

My religious decision was to reject religion. I still believed in a higher power; after all, how can you believe in your own existence if you don't believe in a higher plane? Religion seemed so deceptive though, and so much of it seemed ridiculous. So was Jesus white, or was he more likely dark skinned? And King James, he rewrote the Bible, right? And heaven and hell? Santa Claus? The Easter Bunny? A pregnant virgin?

If psychedelics did one thing for me, it made me form this belief that I'd just wait until death to see what was really true. It seemed like everyone was wrong; no one really knows what happens to us after we die. The world seemed to be organized on speculation and superstition. Like most of my peers, I was conscious of something bigger, but not religious.

I had to respect religion though, at least Catholicism because it helped form who I was, and if I believed one thing, I believed I was a good person, or at least trying to be. No priests ever tried to molest me, and the worst thing that ever happened to me at church was that I was bored out of my mind.

The great outdoors, the great desert, that was my church. Mother

Nature was God. I had absolutely nothing "figured out." But, I'd seen the face of death several times, and I had no fear of Jesus judging me for what I'd done, or not done. In fact, the whole concept seemed ridiculous. In the same breath though, I felt guilty for expressing that, because in the beginning, I was raised Catholic, and Catholic guilt would stick with me a lot longer than any of the beliefs, which is why I probably became a writer; a conversation back and forth in your head is one thing, and it can turn you into a crazy person. Put that conversation down on paper, and you can become a writer, and when people agree with you, or at a minimum, respect you, then you find your readers.

Hopefully your writing is good enough that even those who don't agree with you will read, and that's what America is all about at its *best*, right? A bunch of people who think differently but find common ground in the fact that we are all Americans, and we unite in our differences. Ah, still reaching...

Chapter 6

Different, but privileged.

In my younger twenties, I felt like a freak a lot of the time. I felt lonely. I felt like the only times I really had answers to my questions were when I was out in nature climbing and when I had someone to share that with. Books provided so much too. To know that I wasn't the only one looking for answers, and to know I wasn't the only one critical of religions and institutions. The most influential two authors I read were Jack Kerouac and Martin Luther King Jr.

Kerouac provided the beatnik platform for adventure and the great American road, while King reinforced all the best aspects of Christianity and showed how much could be accomplished with strict adherence to one's moral compass. King was my hero, and Kerouac was my cautionary tale. Kerouac would lead you to the road, and you were on your own once you got there. King could lead you to the proverbial mountaintop. Their books were my buddies. I loved to read and write, and write based on the inspiration of what I'd read.

What I didn't realize then, perhaps because of my deep affection for the "dirtbag" life—although we always used the term climbing bum then—was that this lifestyle, at least in the United States, was an extension of white privilege. Ignorance is bliss, and knowledge is power, right?

As a climbing bum, I accepted that nature was my home, and even if a rock was my pillow, I was where I belonged. But, could I have lived this lifestyle—if I were not white?

It was a difficult question to pose because most the other climbing bums were white. And, at that time, male. Climbing had always seemed like an open-minded community, but it was also the whitest sport in the damn country. And, why was that?

Well, we gloss over it when we learn history; shit, we don't even gloss it over—we flat out lie. We are a nation built upon slavery and genocide. America committed genocide against the Native Americans and enslaved Africans. Any and every history lesson should begin right there. Not with Columbus sailing the ocean blue in 1492 or the pilgrims landing on Plymouth Rock, but with the truth.

My generation grew up with Martin Luther King Jr. as a hero. The context of why he was a hero was vague, at least when you're in seventh grade, as it's difficult to understand for a young white child who was fed a certain narrative about the country. But he was placed there on that pedestal, and the more you learn about King, the more you learn about our country. And the more you admire King, the more you want truth. And, the truth shall set you free.

I grew up with kids of all races, and not much was made of race in my family. I never heard my parents say anything racist, ever, and thus I was not encouraged to be racist. Our neighborhood looked like a lot of middle-class American neighborhoods, with proof that this country could function as the melting pot that we are—whateverthefuck melting pot means. That's the word in my brain for America, I guess.

And, I think my upbringing in this diverse environment made me believe in the virtue that we are all created equal. However, the more you live life and the more you study America, the more you see the playing field is not fair. White privilege is murky, it can be hard to see, but it is real, and it certainly played in my favor when I was just tramping around America and in the desert, roaming as free as I wanted to be.

Looking honestly at America is the only way to move forward. The more I learned of the truth and the more I learned of the problems of the world, the more I dropped out from it, content to be a climbing bum. That's privilege. I had the option to do that, and so I did. For years, in my writing, I romanticized this climbing-bum life, and I think I always will. And why is that?

Well, I suppose, first and foremost, it's because I love the life. But what does living that life do to enhance the world? I don't think anything, really. Then why did the urge to live the climbing-bum lifestyle feel like *everything*? Like the thing I had to do above everything else?

It was freedom, and that American love for it, but, damn, it's really a human thing and not an American thing. Just American branding of freedom. Like stupid fucking country songs. And it was the magic of nature. Land that Native Americans cared for and lived off of in a free society before the first amendment ever came along. And a country that was built largely by African Americans, against their will. A system that also practically enslaves poor whites through economic injustice, and then the Republicans still get their votes by blaming their problems on immigrants. A country that is led today by a white supremacist. That's not fun at all to read, is it?

Fun. The movement that created the dirtbag was largely motivated by fun. At least in all my research that's how I have come to see it. For all intents and purposes, Kerouac and his buddy Neal Cassady were the grandfathers and godfathers of this lifestyle. *On The Road* would get you on the road, but it was *Dharma Bums* where Kerouac seemed to be comfortable in his own skin.

Kerouac killed himself with alcohol. I'd like to think that if he'd found something like rock climbing, he could have saved himself from himself. Ah, still reaching. You're out there still, aren't you, Kerouac? I'm still learning from your lessons, thinking that the answer is out there somewhere, in America.

Chapter 7

Writing about The Desert should be simple, but in America, a simple narrative tells lies, and I don't want to tell no lies, not for romanticism, not for beatnikism, not for dirtbagism.

Every American's life is shaped by religion, war, race, gender, and circumstance. By circumstance, I never went to war, I did not find a religion to embrace, and my race and gender never hindered me. And it was under these conditions that I became an American climber and discovered the magic of the desert.

Perhaps the greatest appeal to the adventurous soul of the desert is the fact that the climbing has only really been relatively safe since the invention of the cam. That bad boy came into the world in 1978, the same year I did, so the modern desert climbing experience was born when I was.

Thus, we have another barrier to writing about the simple life in the desert, and that is gear, which is not simple, or inexpensive, at all.

The dirtbag life had its requirements, and to adequately meet those requirements, you needed something. Dollar dollar bills, y'all. Dead presidents.

This so-called simple life required expensive materials. Sure you could do without them, but no one in the climbing world liked a mooch or a freeloader. Bringing something to the table in climbing is essential. It wasn't like being a dirty hippie—having nothing was not prized for climbers. If anything, the more you brought to the table, the more you were valued.

We needed gasoline, absolutely essential to get from point A to point

B. Thankfully, our government subsidizes petroleum. We thought about climate change and discussed it, but we hadn't been given much of an option for alternative fuels that don't release as much carbon dioxide (or any at all). Something about the government being in bed with the oil industry, I guess. As long as gas was cheap, the dirtbags would hardly think twice about multiple fill-ups to traverse the country just to climb rocks.

Gear. We need it, gotta have it, like a heroin addict needs a needle. Ropes, oh nylon ropes, the best damn technological breakthrough for climbing that came out of World War II, they are like bombproof spider webs, ensuring we'll stay glued to the wall; they won't break—plummeting us to our deaths—unlike the twine and hemp versions that preceded it. Gotta have that nylon, baby!

Aluminum, hmmmm…gotta have that too for our carabiners. Steel, as well, for those anchors. Magnesium carbonate for those sweaty palms. Rain jackets with Gore-Tex. Synthetic clothes made from polypropylene. Specific shoes made with rubber. Tents, sleeping bags, stoves, headlamps, helmets, coolers, iPhones, iPods, iCrashPads…iNeed it all.

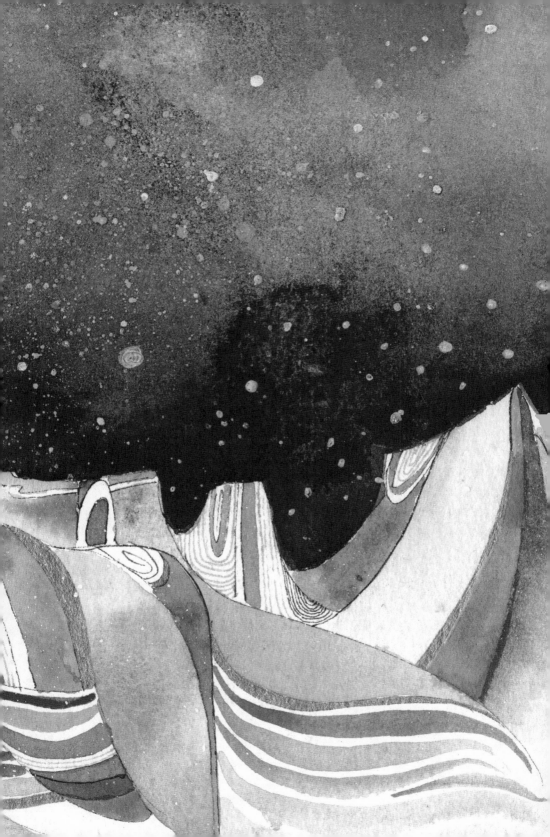

Chapter 8

My college years in The Desert were adventurous and crazy, a complete immersion in the unknown. After I graduated, I began to roam from climbing area to climbing area, and The Desert seemed like just another destination on the circuit.

It was in that era that the inevitable plateau began for me on that Colorado Plateau. I was mostly a dropout from society, and climbing and living in a tent was as much a default as it was my passion.

When I began my life on the road as a climber, destinations became the major ones, not just the proverbial backyard places like Escalante Canyon and Colorado National Monument. When I landed in the desert, I usually landed in Indian Creek.

The Creek had an ease and charm to it. Like Escalante, it was located on BLM land. There were also several conservation easements between the ranchers and the Nature Conservancy, hard work and compromises created so that the public could enjoy the land.

I was enjoying it and calling it home for the time being, college degree in recreation and environmental studies earned, living in a fresh, brand-new tent in the Bridger Jacks camping area.

The Bridger Jacks, eight towers in a row, ranging from a 150 to 400 feet, were quintessentially Indian Creek, only in the realm of being iconic. While most of Indian Creek crack climbing borders on perfection, these towers had only a few perfect splitter cracks.

As for eye candy, they set a perfect backdrop. There was the Easter Island tower, aptly named with no further description required, and then there was the King of Pain, a monster of a tower that appeared to have a cherry on top in the form of a giant boulder, eroded, waiting for time to come along and add it to the talus below.

Who wouldn't want a backyard like that? A lot of climbers did, and despite the bumpy road back there, the campsites were mostly full, so I settled on a corner site, not at all appealing, not a tree for shade, but still a corner to erect my new tent.

Mark was the first to find me for a climb. He was one of many partners I had from college—in fact, the greatest gifts I think my college experience brought me were good friends and adventure partners. After all, my plan was to live rich, on a cheap budget. A competent, safe partner was the very first ingredients on the list for this recipe.

In those years, from time to time, I'd end up with some random partners, and occasionally it would work out, but I always found something was missing. It's kind of like sex—sure, you *could* just hook up with a random, but doing it with someone you knew ensured it would be more meaningful, safe, and enjoyable. Needless to say, I'm not an orgy guy.

I was led to believe, innocently and naïvely, that, simply stated, most climbers were like me, and I would get along with them. But the more I climbed with random people and experienced the climbing community, the more I wanted to only climb with my trusted friends. It's kind of like a job, and there needs to be a résumé showing one spent years learning the basics and the fundamentals from mentors. Many modern climbers seriously lack this, and when they go climbing, it shows.

The things that bothered me about climbing with the randoms were always the unnecessary risks: like people who don't check their knots, belays, or harnesses before venturing up into the vertical; or those that haven't mastered the craft of placing protection but think that they have; or those that half-heartedly belay, as if the rope were a fishing line on a drunken weekend afternoon.

I trusted Mark with my life, no doubt. Mark had also given me a tremendous amount of perspective on life. Two years before this climb I'm going to tell you about, he had a battle with cancer and went through surgery, radiation treatment, and chemotherapy. And all through this, he never stopped climbing. Shortly after finishing chemo back East, he returned to the West and went straight for Medicine Man in Colorado National Monument and sent the crux pitch, yelling, "Fuck you, cancer," when he reached the belay.

Mark also gave me writing fodder by being such a brave, inspiring soul. My first creative essay that was published in a major magazine, the *Mountain Gazette*, was written about him and our adventures together. I'd originally written it out by hand during breaks at my restaurant gig at a coffee shop. At the time, I didn't know if my friend would survive, so it was written with tears and heart, savoring the memories and the moments. He'd also confirmed the truth that life is precious, and time is limited. We all know that, but until we *feel* it, that truth is hard to absorb into the soul. Once you know it, feel it, and experience it, well, it's then I think the real l-i-v-i-n-g happens. The thing about climbing is that it's this delicate edge one tries to dance upon, and as Kelly Cordes says, if you're not living on the edge, you're taking up too much room, right? There are the unavoidable risks, just like driving a car, but then there are the risks we can control. I knew for sure that those partners I danced with took these risks seriously, and I did not want to dance with those who did not.

We sought Powders of Persuasion on the Bridger Jack Butte, the rightmost "tower" on the formation, famous for a hand crack that was supposed to be a full two-hundred-foot rope length. That dihedral was obviously visible from camp, but the rest of the climb appeared to be a mystery. From experience, I knew the cap rock would be loose, a layer of deteriorating sandstone, out of character in a climbing area known for its perfect rock and cracks.

We were lured in by the long hand crack, which seemed like something to see, to experience; I imagined pure bliss, perfect jams, way high off the deck, poetry in motion. Of course, this is climbing, and it is never as one anticipates.

This long corner was guarded by a chimney that was not at all sexy or appealing. It was a pitch to get to the next pitch. I climbed up, approached a death block that hovered in the chimney, and downclimbed right back to the belay. The success of the climb was now in Mark's hands. Did he want to go up and check it out, or bail and head to the Splitterville that surrounded us?

Mark wasn't giving up without a proper fight, and off-width/chimney climbing could easily be compared to a fight. Your hands are all taped up, and you're ready to accept cuts and bruises in order to be successful. Soon enough, Mark was on the sharp end and masterfully climbed up to the death block and positioned himself around it, using some sort of Houdini technique that I had not considered. It was as if he magically positioned himself around the boulder, careful not to touch it, with the prospect of dislodging it straight onto me. With that magical movement, he set us up for success, and we were now below the epic-hand-crack corner.

That was just like Mark. I would have been fine with bailing and going to a crag with perfect splitters all around, but he found a way to make it happen. And then we could finally experience this dihedral that we'd been staring at all the years we camped in the Bridger Jacks.

The pitch was a powerful piece of geometry and geology, nearly two hundred feet of perfect verticality. It packed a punch similar to many pitches I'd done in Indian Creek. At first it seemed easy, jamming hands and feet into the crack, but then the pump started to kick in, and I was afraid I'd fall. The equation was so simple, but the physiology was not. But as I got pumped out, I demanded myself to rise to the occasion of this feature, and I managed not to fall out, focusing on my breathing and thinking positive thoughts. When I finished the pitch, that very familiar adrenaline wash came over my brain, and I collapsed into a puddle of satisfaction at the belay. I was as one with the desert as one can get, well, at least until we are dust ourselves.

We still had two pitches to go, and the rock got worse as we went up. Near the top, on the sharp end again, I went twenty some feet without gear, using that technique of balance and prayer on delicate sandstone edges and holds, just waiting for that break when I would go plummeting down to the marginal gear I'd snuck into some horizontal cracks.

On the top was an epic view of sandstone for miles, and then a strange sight, a copy of the Book of Mormon with burned pages in some vain attempt at a fire. What the hell was going on there I'll probably never know, but it represented the hedonistic aspect of climbing. These days, I'd clean something like that up, trash on sacred ground. That particular day, we were too worried about how we'd get down. The rappel anchors were less than ideal but passed our test of redundancy and safety. The pioneers of the desert seemed to think little about long-term use of their anchors, or, they simply just didn't have the quality of bolts and hangers that we have now. Many bolts, pitons, and anchors were like land mines left from a long-forgotten battle. Hanging off tattered, sun-bleached webbing, we vowed to come back someday and fix that.

Mark left the desert soon after this, on to a guiding gig in the Northwest.

In college, that was supposed to be my career too. I loved climbing, so why wouldn't it be a perfect job? But, I soon realized I didn't have the nerves or patience for guiding. Holding my climbing partner's life in my hands that I knew well was enough for me; being responsible for a beginner who was a stranger gave me too much anxiety. Guiding is tough, blue-collar work, and it was another thing I admired Mark for. Still, I wondered if I'd made a mistake by not following that path. I was just washing dishes for a living, the same damn job I had when I was sixteen. I got a paycheck now and again for freelance writing, but they were few and far between; writing was more of a hobby than a job.

Just as Mark rolled out, some more friends rolled in. Dave was on a similar schedule and life path as Mark, getting some desert climbing in before guiding season really kicked off. Dave was guiding on Denali in Alaska. He seemed to savor the dirt and absence of snow as much as the climbing. It would be rough, as the season in Colorado went from winter to spring, to then go up high, back to winter in Alaska, even though it's the summer. Dave was easy to please in the desert, and he had a certain vibe of contentment, always, there. He made me feel at ease.

Dave was one of those all-American guys. He often lived like a dirtbag but always seemed to be clean-shaven and smell like soap. As a teenager with a single mother, he started to go down the path of a troubled youth, but then an Outward Bound trip showed him the glories of the outdoors. He'd joke that NOLS (National Outdoor Leadership School) stood for "nerds out losing shit," but deep down, we knew organizations like that saved lives and made lives worth living because of nature, like his.

When his mother needed a liver transplant, he offered to have the surgery for her. A massive scar across his belly shows his love for his mom and his unequivocal dedication to always doing the right thing.

His voice is even quintessentially American, in the best of ways, kind of like he's a beloved radio host. I used to think it was just a fun thing he did, until I heard him call his mom one day when we were on a climbing trip, and he talked to her in the very same voice. "Hey, Mom, your son Dave here, coming at you from Zion National Park, a true American treasure. How the heck are you?"

Dave smoothed out the edges in our ragtag, dirtbag crew and made it all seem wholesome. He never liked the crowds much and, in his heart, was always more of an old-school climber, doing it for the satisfaction and the silence, for the sake of the song.

Tim had shown up just when Dave did. Another buddy from college, who, like Dave, had a career in the outdoors and wasn't just aimlessly floating like I was. He lived in Monticello, the closest town to Indian Creek, and ran a youth outdoor corps.

Tim was one of the first people I met in Gunnison and one of those people I knew I'd be friends with right off the bat. He clearly liked fun, and he also didn't shy away from tough topics of conversation. Just a couple months into our friendship, he told me about his father committing suicide when he was a teenager.

Tim and I have been through a lot together, and I've watched him go from the guy who could easily drink a twelve-pack to quitting drinking altogether. He's the leader of our Indian Creek crew. His friendliness could be described as legendary; people never forget meeting Tim, and sometimes at the crag, he's a bit of a celebrity.

The definitive quality about Tim as a climber is his love for ice climbing. He loves Indian Creek through and through and has dedicated countless hours to trail building, elaborate campfire parties, and new routing, but somehow, even on a hot summer day, he'll turn the conversation to ice climbing. It's a skill of his.

Name the topic: Russian collusion in our presidential race?

"Oh, man, I hear Russia's got some great ice climbing…"

Global warming?

"Oh, that's going to be bad for ice climbing…"

Did you watch the World Series?

"Oh the World Series, that means ice climbing season is just around the corner…did I tell you about this route me and Smokey Joe did in the Black Canyon last season? It was epic…"

Tim can simply turn any conversation into talking about ice climbing. He loves ice climbing more than anyone I've ever met, as if he were an ambassador for frozen water. He views everyone he meets as a future friend, and once you've got Timmy's approval, well, you're in the crew.

The day Tim and Dave arrived, I was taking a rest day, so I did what you do in Indian Creek: I left them a message on the Beef Basin message board just off the highway and told them what my plans were.

My rest day was like any other rest day: showering, stocking up on beer and food, checking my email, writing in my journal, calling the parents, stuff like that. Once I'd done everything I needed to do, I headed back home to my campsite. As I rolled in, I realized something wasn't right.

My brand-new tent, my home, was flattened. My heart sank when I saw the sight. My brand-new tent, trampled and crushed to oblivion, and the contents of the cooler spilled out into what appeared to me was an act of vandalism. I looked around to find the culprit. Then, I looked to the ground and saw hoofprints. Horses. It was horses.

Anger mixed with disbelief. There were many places where it's downright stupid to leave food out in a cooler, but The Creek is not one of those places. We always leave our coolers out.

Further inspection revealed the horses had eaten some of the carrots I had in my cooler, and they even drank a couple beers!

Dave and Tim quickly arrived on the scene. I expected sympathy, but all they did was laugh and make fun of me.

They did, however, secure a better spot in the campground, and I quickly moved in, happy to get out of the campsite that would be forever known as the spot where "the horse incident" occurred.

It was then that I moved into a new tent. Dave had an extra that he'd stashed away in his truck, for times like this. As he described it, each detail seemed to be better than the next: "You're in luck. I have this extra tent that I scored on Denali last year," he started.

"It's a high-end mountaineering model, probably retailed around a thousand bucks," Dave continued. "These clients just left it behind after their expedition, said they didn't want it anymore, and my boss said I could have it.

"There's just one catch," he said.

"And…?" I asked.

"Well, there were a lot of bad storms on their trip. So the guys started, you know, relieving themselves in the vestibule."

"As in shitting?" I inquired.

"Yeah," Dave said, with his face still deadpan. "Then the storm got really bad. So the one guy just started taking care of business in the tent. And one time he missed."

"He missed?" I asked.

"He missed," he answered. "He missed the bag. And, a little bit got on the tent. That's how I got it. I cleaned it out with bleach and aired it out for days. It's good to go, man."

An awkward silence fell upon us.

"It's better than nothing," Dave said convincingly.

"Better than nothing," I repeated. "Well, I guess I don't have a ton of options right now."

"It's clean," he said. "I used bleach."

"Well…shit, I guess I'm moving into the Shit Tent," I declared.

Chapter 9

I can vividly remember the horses, the crushed tent, and even the teeth marks on the carrots. I remember being at camp with Tim and Dave, but for the life of me, I don't remember what we were climbing or where we were climbing. Perhaps I was just lost at sea or, I suppose, lost in the desert. Whatever I climbed has blended into time, my memory a talus field, a castle that eventually becomes sand.

It was this time that I was just as much of a hopeless romantic, a poet, as I was a climber. And everything I'm aware of about myself then, I wasn't much aware of at the time.

I was empty in many ways because I had ended up following the path of my heroes, who were the cautionary tales. I was following Kerouac and Garcia down their philosophical rabbit hole, but why was I not following Dr. Martin Luther King Jr.? Kerouac killed himself with alcohol, and Jerry killed himself with heroin and other drugs. In many ways, they had been devoured by the following they created. Kerouac couldn't handle the fame, neither could Jerry. King was the only hero of mine who had died a hero's death.

In college, I'd pondered becoming an activist, but I never did. The lonely road to climbing was the only path I really followed. I wanted to be a writer, but I did not write much at all.

The climbing community and the land housed me well. I was lonely, traveling from place to place, but when I arrived, I always had friends. Friends that were aware of the risks of climbing and danced with it how I preferred to dance. I was doing little to honor my hero Dr. King, but I think I was honoring Kerouac and Garcia, by simply existing in this counterculture lifestyle and not being totally self-destructive. I was not part of the "lame America," as Jerry put it. I did inherit white privilege, something I never gave one thought to then, but now as I contemplate those days, so much of it comes back to that.

I didn't write much, but I did write, and I thought about writing all the time, which of course is nothing if you don't do something about it.

I always knew I wanted to give something to the world. King, Kerouac, and Garcia all gave their lives in one way or another. King died like Jesus did. Kerouac died so sadly. Garcia was engulfed by heroin and the monster that had become The Grateful Dead. How would I die, and when I died, would anyone remember what I had given?

I knew a few things there, post college, lost but attached to the climbing world. I knew I did not want to die anytime soon. That may seem like common sense, but I also get the feeling that there are those who live life so close to the edge that they can become indifferent to when death takes them. This may be conscious or unconscious. I had been close to wanting to die when I was suicidal and twenty; I had almost died a couple times after that when I was just learning to climb and wanting to live. I knew three things: I wanted to live, I wanted to climb, and I wanted to write.

And I wanted to exist in all of the Americas I grew to know. I wanted to live in King's dream of America, where we judge one another on the content of our character and not the color of our skin; I wanted to exist in that beatnik, fuck-you-to-conformity America; and I wanted to live in the Grateful Dead America, from "spending a night in Utah in a cave up in the hills" to "the future is here, we are it, we are on our own."

Plateauing on the Colorado Plateau was seemingly teaching me nothing, so I'd go back to the mountains in the state of Colorado when I got tired of it. I rarely wrote about the desert and found it to be a place between other places. Yosemite thrilled me more; the Black Canyon stirred up epics for breakfast; Joshua Tree seemed to be more of a place to call home than my backyard desert. Indian Creek and the desert were places I'd just be from time to time, infinite in their space, but the spirits rarely spoke to me, or perhaps I was just not listening.

My life continued for a few years like this. In that space of time, I knew I'd never become an activist. Wars continued, and I did not protest. Environmental injustice continued, and I did not protest. Economic injustice continued, and I did not protest.

I did continue to write. I still wrote infrequently, but later when I had tendonitis in my elbows and wondered if climbing would still be a thing I'd do, I got a writing gig, a PR job at the college in Gunny. I learned the craft, and I appreciated the craft. I became a total square and hardly visited The Desert anymore. I figured my future was in writing and not climbing.

I lost my gig, partly due to the economic crash and partly due to the fact that I was burnt out on the nine-to-five life. They cut my job to half time, so I quit. Something about me was angry and upset, and there was this other part of me that was joyously singing on the inside. Kind of like in the movie *Office Space* when the main character starts saying *fuck it*, and things start going his way.

This was right around when Obama got elected. I was fed up with George W. and his ignorant ways (and wars), and I rejoiced when Obama became president. Soon after though, I was unemployed and broke and realized that when you're jobless and moneyless, it don't really matter who the damn president is.

The end of this chapter in my life, the one that I thought I could be happy writing at a nine-to-five, surrounded by walls, drove me closer to the desert, with absolutely no intention to be closer to the desert. I just wanted out. I moved from Gunnison to Durango on a whim, with nothing more than an editor from the local weekly telling me I could write freelance for them. As any freelance writer knows, writing for a local indie paper ain't good for much in the bank account, but it's good to get to know a community. That was my plan, which wasn't much of a thought-out plan; it was more of an escape route.

It was just weeks into this move that I realized just how much closer I was to Indian Creek, that old friend. It didn't take long for us to get reacquainted. I had changed. It had mostly remained the same, save for its ever-increasing popularity.

I was back in the desert, and, maybe, just maybe, I was reading to start listening to the desert.

Alas, before we go further into the rabbit hole of the desert, before the spirits start speaking, and before I paint my canvas, a few more influencers in my life and my art are worth looking at.

Ed Abbey is a good one to start with. Abbey was never a hero for me, and really only a small portion of his writing spoke to me. The writing that did, *Desert Solitaire*, well, that changed my life, and good books have that power.

Desert Solitaire is a simple book, written when Abbey was a ranger in Arches National Park in the 1950s, a feisty tribute to loving the freedom and openness of the desert and lamenting any "improvements" that made it easier for the mainstream tourists to access it. It's a beautiful book, poetry for hundreds of pages, a primer for loving a land that will never love you back. Like Kerouac's books, it's easy to criticize as boring, too simple, not enough action, but everything can be criticized, and those that critique can rarely create.

Abbey was an icon out West, a household name to those who loved the desert and felt a calling to protect it. He was long dead by the time I was in college, yet his name carried weight. "Have you read *Desert Solitaire*?" has been uttered by thousands upon thousands, and accompanied by "a look" that says if you haven't read it, you ought to.

George Sibley was our Ed Abbey over in Gunnison. He was my college professor and advisor to our student newspaper. George never gained the fame that Abbey did, but around town, he was regarded as highly as Abbey was nationally. He was an army dropout who settled in Crested Butte in a unique period of time when the hippies were coming in and the miners were still there. His writing of that era is some of my favorite writing of all time. He understood the complexities of the West and mountain-town living. He loathed the lameness of mainstream America and wanted to live the rest of his days in the mountains.

I loved Sibley's stories, so when he would praise my work in our newspaper meetings, my confidence for writing soared; I never knew what I wanted to be when I grew up, but he helped me see that I would become a writer. Older writers and editors have such a power in their hands when they interact with younger writers. A lot of that has been broken down now with so much self-publishing, or independent publishing as I like to call it. Self-publishing sounds like masturbating to me, like you couldn't get someone else to do it, so you do it yourself. Indie publishing sounds like a *fuck you* to mainstream publishing: I'm going to do my own damn thing and be more successful than I would have if I would have teamed up with you.

George always lifted me up instead of bringing me down, though my submissions were always heavily marked up with the basic grammatical errors because I never learned that stuff until later. Other editors would "piss all over my work," as they used to say, and I'd hold a grudge against them for that. George would ground me with grammatical critique but always let me soar as high as I wanted in creativity and joy.

George once told me my work reminded him of Kerouac, which could have been a lie; maybe he just wanted to encourage me, but the day he told me that was one of the most important days of my life, because it meant maybe I could live like Kerouac—wild and free on the open road. He also told me to let my writing really sing, some of the best damn advice I've ever gotten.

Of course, Kerouac couldn't even live like Kerouac; it was an illusion, and I later learned that he would write in these twenty-thousand-word bursts fueled by speed. That kind of writing can't be good for the writer's heart or soul, but damn, it did provide some good stories; I guess one just wants their heroes to enjoy themselves. (Later, I learned that Kerouac had originally inspired Jerry Garcia; inspiration can go a long way.)

Kerouac, Abbey, and Sibley all held their own place in the hearts of their readers (and their coffee tables), and that space seemed just as sacred as the experiences and places they would write about. All held Mother Nature as the highest of high. I wanted to walk in their footsteps.

My purpose was met with clarity when, years down the road after deciding to become a real writer, people told me my work influenced them. I wanted to make an impact in the world, and I'd failed in so many ways. All modern Americans are "takers" in one way or another, and the longer I live, the more I'm aware how I take, but it was the greatest of all pleasures to be a "giver."

Slowly but surely, I realized the more I cut down walls and gave my soul to the reader, the more I was being true to the craft. Sure, some folks didn't like my style, but the reality is the more people who read and appreciate your work, the more people there are who are not going to dig it. In the end though, you remember the love letters more than the internet comments.

I realized, over time, I had the opportunity to influence people the way Kerouac and company influenced me; moments in the past when I'd wondered what the purpose of all these lonely days on the road were about suddenly transformed into something important. As long as I would write honestly about my wins and losses, I was on my life's path, and nothing short of death would take that from me.

As one gains a reputation for their work, certain things are said about that person. And while I don't have the luxury of being a fly on the wall when people are talking about my work, I've heard some entertaining things. One of my favorites came from my friend Jonathan who once had a buddy say, "Oh yeah, that guy Luke, the one who is always writing about his girlfriends."

And it was true I had a penchant for freely writing about dating, and I was a hopeless romantic. Like Willie Nelson singing about his loneliness on the road, I did the same in my stories. Climbers, we often don't want to settle down until later, but like any other human, we want company. Some of my climbing stories probably read like sappy country songs, but I think it resonated with people, because everyone gets their heart broken a time or two—it makes us stronger. Can you know love if you never lose it?

The more I wrote, the more people reached out to me and told me I inspired them or I was able to write about things that they had felt too. And, the more I wrote, the more people on the internet would tell me I was a total amateur and didn't know what the hell I was doing as a writer.

Here's feedback from two different readers on the exact same book, *American Climber*:

One reviewer said: *I just finished your book,* American Climber. *I have never been so indulged into a book. I absolutely loved reading about your story. From growing up in the Midwest trying to find yourself to accomplishing the biggest goal of a climber, summiting El Cap. I enjoyed how you expressed yourself and everything you went through in life. I really appreciate you sharing your story, I learned a lot about life through your book.*

And another said: *This was some of the most tedious, repetitious, immature writing I have struggled through. Then the never-ending dialog about relationships, everyone goes through that, you're a writer! Make it interesting or leave it out. As a climber the descriptions of the various climbing experiences were average and allowed me to get through the book but that was it. Compared to other climbing literature this is below average and worth skipping.*

I know, as humans, we have a tendency to be drawn toward negative feedback, but both the positive feedback and the negative feedback inspired me. Negative reviews and feedback are inevitable, but if I knew I wrote from the heart and believed in the story, even negative feedback inspired me, in a strange way. It lit a fire, and the fire kept on a burning. So I just kept on a writing.

Chapter 10

My arrival to living near The Desert came along with a dry spell in the weather. Durango seemed like a tropical paradise compared to Gunnison. I was used to hunkering down in the winter and escaping to the desert for a few precious hours in the dirt when I could. This was different, just different.

I had bouts of fear and doubt in town, wondering where the hell I'd work given that the economy was total shit at the time, if I'd ever meet the woman of my dreams, and if I'd even make it in this idyllic but pricey town. Fear can be a motivator, but I think everyone needs a break from fear. So in the midst of establishing myself in this new, charming town on the edge of the desert and the mountains, I went climbing.

My two best friends named Tim were in tow. Two Tent Timmy was visiting from Oregon, and my "other best friend named Tim" had moved to Durango the very same month that I had. Tim and I were both unemployed. Indian Creek for a few warm winter days was the perfect place to be.

Tim was in the process of getting clean from the bottle. I'd watched him struggle with alcohol for years, and one morning after a rough night of taking care of him out on the town, I sat him down and told him I didn't think we could be friends anymore if he continued drinking. He did continue drinking and got into a horrific car accident when he was intoxicated. The cops said it was a miracle he was alive and they had to use the Jaws of Life device to get him out of the vehicle.

Tim's life seemed to happen like this; it was one of several stories I'd heard of him using up his nine lives. I felt bad for Tim and knew he wanted to be rid of the demons of alcoholism. Everyone around Tim wanted him to quit too, but that sort of thing has to come from the inside. Changing ain't easy, and most people don't change. Tim was/is special though. I was rooting for him; I was also mentally prepared for the worst, but he's one of those people that found the inner strength to overcome his addiction.

Two Tent had been my rock. We grew up in Illinois together and attended the same church at seven years old. He was always there when I needed him to be, and climbing with him was always sacred. He held the torch of trad climbing high, and every adventure with Tim was a good adventure. He had a gold tooth that shined in the sun.

We had all of Indian Creek to ourselves; no one else was in the Superbowl, which had a blanket of snow covering it. We were freezing cold in the morning, huddling by the fire, but by midday, when we were at the crag, we basked in a solar oven created by the sun on varnished rock. Maybe it was that contrast in the environment that has made this day stand out so much—snow on the valley floor with a striking-blue sky overhead. Or maybe it was the contrast in my mind state—worry, worry, worry about what's going to happen in this new stage of life, and then being in the desert and not being worried about anything really, other than staying warm and staying safe. Whatever the reason, this memory shines through like a ray of sunshine in a dark canyon.

While Tim and Two Tent warmed up, I roamed the Broken Tooth Wall freely, going on a little hike and basking in this warmth that felt so divine. I took some photos of them from afar and then hiked to the far-right side to see if I could maybe find some unclimbed cracks. In all my years of climbing in Indian Creek, I'd never put up a new route, but I'd always wanted to.

Sure enough, as I walked around that bend, I found several unclimbed cracks on the far right side of the wall, just enough off the beaten path that no one had gotten around to putting them up yet. I took pictures of one particular line that looked good and zoomed in to the top to see if I could see any evidence of anchors. Nothing. I ran back to Two Tent and Tim and excitedly told them about my findings. I asked them if they would be game to give the line a go, and they were. I ran back down to the car to get a bolt kit I always had stashed away, mostly for replacing bad anchors. Looking at my stash of bolts revealed I didn't have the right size—the bolts I had were made for bomber granite, too small for sandstone. The new line would have to wait.

My life started revolving around this routine of getting settled in Durango and then escaping back to the desert. This empty, quiet, wintery desert was a side of Indian Creek I'd never seen before, and it was my favorite side. The sky seemed bluer, the rocks redder, and with fewer people around, it felt wilder. We climbed with the place all to ourselves and watched the ravens fly.

Soon enough, Two Tent and I returned to that line I wanted to establish. I wrote about the experience in an early issue of *The Climbing Zine*:

When Two Tent comes back through Durango, it takes absolutely no convincing to venture out to The Creek again. What else would we do with our lives? We caravan out West toward our beloved red-rock desert in the middle of the week. The Superbowl campsite is empty again. In the busy season, we're always scrambling to find a site; in the deep of winter, I almost hope there're other climbers present for some company. Alas, it's just my best friend and me.

Armed with longer bolts for sandstone, I convince Two Tent to check out the unclimbed line on the right side of Broken Tooth. After a warm-up, we head over to the line, which I consider naming after his gold front tooth, the result of a nasty break-dancing accident years ago. I figure the name would be appropriate for the wall.

The line starts in somewhat loose rock, with protection in a crack that's about half an inch wide. Footholds crumble off as I climb up and down the rock. Quickly, I resort to aid climbing, as the climb turns a small roof into a flare, the crack just larger than an inch. Two Tent settles into the despair of a long lead belay as I aid through this section and then a hundred-foot-long off-width that looms above.

Suddenly, I'm not excited at all about the possibility of a first ascent, as I have Two Tent send up all our off-width gear on a tag line. There's a reason the pursuit of first ascents has mostly faded at The Creek; more often than not, they involve off-width, and for the average suitor, a new route takes most of the day, with one person struggling above and the other in another kind of sufferfest, a long belay. Why do this when you could be climbing perfect splitters, one after the other, all day long?

I go into a mode of climbing and prayer as I fit my body in the off-width for inches of upward progress. I curse myself for the pursuit as I put my off-width skills to the test—knees on one side of the crack, heels and toes on the other, my arms chicken-winged into the crack, my entire body covered with dust, from head to toe. Two Tent sends up occasional words of encouragement, the only remainder of the positive and optimistic notions I had before starting up. Ninety feet up the off-width section, I place my last piece of big gear, a green #3 Big Bro. I worm up and finally reach a hand crack, jamming it until I reach a spot to place anchors. Two Tent sends up the drill kit. I am weak and not psyched to drill the anchors as the sun is quickly fading. Defeated, I sink in two bolts, rappel, and clean the gear, leaving a toprope for my partner. He seconds the route in style with the last rays of light for the day. I'm exhausted as we hike down the trail, relieved to be done with climbing for the day, as the heavy pack sinks into my aching body. The campfire and food restore warmth to the soul.

While we sit next to the campfire, we work on the plaque for our new route, carving the name in with the drill bit. Though I'd considered naming it Gold Tooth after Two Tent's gold tooth, I decided the line was just too brutal and haggard to commemorate my best friend in such a way. After my comrade's approval, we name it Snaggle Tooth.

Ol' Snaggle Tooth could have been a singular pursuit; after all, it wasn't really that enjoyable in the moment, and the route itself wasn't even all that good, not compared to its neighbors. But, right by Snaggle Tooth were several other unclimbed cracks, and after a few weeks, I remembered what I liked about the experience more than what I didn't like.

I was also moving from climbing on mostly granite to climbing on sandstone, and the climber gets used to a certain medium. Granite often seems like a delicate dance, balancing on tiny edges. Wingate-sandstone cracks can be a little more thuggy; all limbs are almost always in the crack. But don't let me bore you with the details—I've just found that once I get really comfortable on one type of rock, I get uncomfortable on another. Years later, I'd lose all my instincts on granite after climbing at The Creek so much. Plus, "getting strong" on one type of rock does not apply to other types. I've seen professional climbers, who succeed on the Ninja Warrior TV show for big money, unable to send a relatively "easy" V4 roof crack in Joshua Tree, while little old me, a comparatively less fit climber, could walk up and do that roof crack without overexerting myself, but they bled all over it and left stumped by the technique and the sequences.

That's not a humble brag, or maybe it is. My point is: strength in rock climbing is so specific, and many climbers that are good climbers are only "good" on certain mediums. More important than that though is how we feel comfortable on the rock, and at this point in my career at The Creek, I still wasn't comfortable, not like I was on granite. Ten years in, I was still a relative newbie.

I couldn't have been more excited for something new to be stoked about. Those winter days also tricked us into thinking we had the desert to ourselves, which I guess we did—we just wouldn't for long. But this desert is so big that you can always have it to yourself if you want to.

Ten years in, hiking the desert, to find new routes, became part of the experience, and thus, the desert became bigger. Some days I would hike by myself, other days with friends. Tim was always game for hiking; he knew this desert well from all his years working there, and he knew how to move about in this desert. *Don't bust the crust, man* is always a rule— avoid stomping on the cryptobiotic soil as much as possible. Stay in the washes when you can. Know when to look around: the remnants of the ancestral Puebloans are all around, from pictographs and petroglyphs to ruins, moki steps, pieces of pottery, and shards from tools, little specs of rock that don't look like they belong in this plateau of sandstone, because, well, they didn't—they came from places far away, from trades with other tribes.

The miners and the ranchers left their marks as well, and they are the reasons we have the roads we have these days. Their remnants are not as interesting or as romantic though, but I guess it depends on which narratives you romanticize. I'm sure the Ancestral Puebloans lived very hard lives out here. It's nearly impossible to imagine what it was like in Indian Creek a thousand years ago. The climate was much different; a major river ran through the zone; they grew corn and lived within the rocks where they could. If I could transport back to any era, I know I would be torn between the 1960s in California and 1060s in what we now call Indian Creek, just to see how they lived and to see if it was as magical as I've romanticized.

Even better than time travel is creating your own life in the manner you'd like to live it, or at least trying to guide it in that direction. So, I made a decision, whether it was conscious or unconscious, that I had to start writing ferociously with discipline and spending as much time in the desert, with my friends, trying to do things that had never been done, while being equally amazed at what had happened a thousand years ago. There's nothing new under the sun—that's for sure—yet there's the thrill of the chase, and there's the unspeakable, why you're drawn to what you are drawn to, why you notice it when you do, even though your steps have perhaps crossed this juncture a hundred times before, how you can find your place, your haven, in a place you once wrote off as inhospitable, wasteland, a stop along the way, how that could become home.

Chapter 11

Now some men will drive to the edges of nothing
So they can take a peek at the great abyss
Some men avoid love like it was a plague or something
So they can leave the seat down when they piss
—John Hiatt, "Ethylene"

Pendulum is a word I've heard a lot lately—used to describe anything from American politics to the range of emotions and experiences in climbing. Writing and climbing have been forever intertwined for me, and they swing together in my inner and outer pendulums. And so has love and the pursuit of romantic love. Love, I would dare say, is always there in climbing, or at least always there when it's a positive climbing experience. And that love can become metaphorical: a great climbing experience can live within one's soul as one of the ultimate adventures of life, love, and Mother Nature.

As I wrote earlier, I had a reputation for being a writer who wrote about his ex-girlfriends and love affairs too much, but that has never been something I've felt apologetic about. After all, I'm a fucking artist—who shall an artist apologize to for those that do not appreciate their art? To write about what other people won't write about in America is perhaps the duty of the prose writer. And that, after all, was who I was, and probably all I would ever be.

All of this can seem inconsequential, but I think it's also my duty to push past the trivial and realize that everything is everything, and all little details matter. And if my existence was simply to write, to love, and to climb, then dammit, I better do that the best I could and make it benefit as many souls as possible.

It was those cold late-November mornings in The Creek when I longed for love the most, longed to have someone next to me in my tent. And in those mornings, love seemed the most impossible. There was love of the community—we gathered and ate and drank and danced—but I longed for the intimate kind of love.

I looked for love in all the wrong places you could say: in women I knew I wasn't compatible with in the long run, too young, too wild, too many kids from too many baby daddies, lived too far away, or simply didn't even like me. That's the curse of the hopeless (hopeful) romantic I suppose: we believe anything is possible, and it is, but we fail to see the obvious at times when there's a chance at love.

And that's how it was this morning, the day after Thanksgiving, when I woke up early as hell in the back of my Subaru, and it was cold, so cold and lonely. I couldn't sleep because I was tormented by the thoughts of unrequited love. This one was too damn young for me, like she grew up watching Harry Potter young, and I grew up on the Care Bears, yet I wanted her and wanted to believe it could work. We'd gone climbing the day before, and I leaned in for a kiss at the end of the day, but she pushed me back. She informed me that she now had a boyfriend back in Boulder where she lived—we had a fling the summer before, and I thought maybe I had another chance because she told me she'd be in The Creek over Thanksgiving. But it was just that friend sort of reaching out, not the reaching out for love.

I sat there cold and alone in my sleeping bag for what seemed like hours, replaying the previous day in my head. I wrote sad thoughts to myself in my journal and kept peeking out for the sun to rise over the bend.

That was love, the sun on my face. That was a fine way to start the day. At Thanksgiving that year, the sun shined all week. We were lucky. The weather seems to either be sunny and perfect that time of year, or terribly rainy, snowy, muddy, foggy—one year, the Mog year, it was muddy and cloudy—or just plain cold. But the sun didn't really improve my mood, so when everyone else went climbing for the day, I decided to go off on my own, take a little hike, get my mind and heart sorted.

So I drove off the highway onto a dirt road and rolled up it for a few miles. Not a soul in sight. Perfect. As I hiked, I started to feel better and less sorry for myself, doing that inner self-talk and realizing it's just another day under the sun in the desert. Things will move on for you. The sun will come out tomorrow. Look at how glorious this life is; look at how beautiful and meaningful and meaningless it all is.

My plan was to hike up to a formation shaped like a submarine that only had a few routes on it, but at the last minute, another wall caught my eye, and I figured I'd hike to a wall that didn't have any documented routes or any information, really. I carefully crawled up the hillside, kicking down loose rocks and trying to avoid busting any crust. Step by step, my mood got better, and it really improved when I got to the wall and found some unclimbed cracks—the goal of any climbing prospector in the desert. Each one I encountered made my heart aflutter, and I couldn't wait to get back to the crew and tell them my findings. Perhaps this would be our own wall to develop; we could paint our own masterpieces.

When I got back into the main canyon, I joined the crew. Tim asked about my hike, and he could see the stoke from the look on my face, and then I sprayed him down about what I'd found. The wall was crowded that day, and I recall an old climber from Gunnison being there and complaining about how busy it was, how he couldn't find anything to climb. I knew him, but he didn't notice me, and he was putting off such a negative vibe I didn't even say hello—plus the contrast of what I'd just found made me laugh; it's all in your mind sometimes—there's always something new around the bend in the desert.

Another warm winter with not a lot of snow followed that Thanksgiving—those seem to be the trend lately in the Southwest—so it wasn't that long until we were back at The Creek. I'd been thinking about that new wall all winter and recruited Tim and our buddy Todd to take a look.

Todd was/is a character. I'd met him through our dear friend Adam Lawton, who died in an avalanche in 2012. He and Adam were best buddies; they skied the wildest lines together, and Todd was understandably devastated by his loss. I never would have known Todd if it weren't for Adam, so every time we hung out, it reminded me of him. Todd is East Coast in his mannerisms, talks with that Massachusetts accent, and has the attitude to match. He is the best runner I've ever met; runs like Forrest Gump, like the wind blows. Adam brought him into our crew, and he fit in quite nicely.

We retraced my steps from the previous November. It's impossible to exactly follow one's steps because though trails do form quite easily in this desert, it still takes many trips for a trail to break in. I was excited about bringing my friends back to this wall—it meant we were one step closer to beginning the development; once they got psyched on the wall, we'd begin the siege.

We told a story or two—Todd told us about saving a guy's life by unburying him in an avalanche (he was on the news and everything)—mixed with giving each other shit and taking a break now and again to look back at the expanse of desert.

It was dry as a bone, only slight traces of snow on the north-facing aspects; the contrast that usually exists this time of year between the white of the snow and the red of the rock and dirt was hardly present. Spring would be on its way in no time, and I was excited by the prospect of a new wall to completely consume me.

By this point, I'd scored a job in a local restaurant. So I would spend my mornings writing and my nights rolling burritos, folding tacos, and cheesing up nachos. It wasn't a bad gig, and I could work whenever I wanted and take off whenever I wanted. The owner was independent minded and was running a wildly successful business; it was one of the busiest places in town. Plus it was based on the concept of healthy, affordable food—I liked that. I could live on just rice and beans if I had to. He even took time out of his days to meet with me and give me business advice for my zine.

I knew my spring, and perhaps many springs and falls to come, would revolve around working to put food on the table and escaping to the desert.

I've never been an aspiring real estate agent, but as we approached the wall, I tried to sell it, showing off all the unclimbed cracks it offered. I was anticipating, in my mind, their response. I knew they were going to love it.

"So...what do you guys think?"

Tim was the first to speak. "It's cool...but..."

"But...?" I asked.

"Well the climbs are far apart, and there're really not good places to hang out," Tim said. "A good wall needs a good hang."

My heart sank a little, but then Tim offered, "There're more walls; look at them. We'll find another good one."

I quickly realized Tim was right, and we retreated to the main canyon to climb a pitch or two before the sun left us for the day. As we geared up, I realized I'd forgotten my harness. Another day spent in the pursuit of nothing—that's climbing for you. Todd realized he had another in his car though—that's climbing for you too: your friends have your back.

It wasn't long before we were hiking walls again in the farthest reaches of the corridor, where there was no one around and it often felt like we were in the pursuit of nothingness. A beautiful, varnished wall, looking just like the other classic walls of the canyon, proved to have little more than a climb or two. Still, we kept hiking.

Later that spring, Tim and I geared up for another exploratory hike in an area that no one had probably explored since the uranium days. If anyone had, it was surely a climber in search of what we were after. A zone where only the cows, lizards, bunnies, and birds were. With the silence though turned a focus on each and every step. I'd see things that I never really saw when I was in the main zone, where there was always human interaction going on. Even if we never found anything, we found a little bit of solitude, a little bit of silence.

That silence quickly comes to a halt when you send a boulder tumbling down the talus and watch it gain speed, knocking off everything in its path. Trundling, we call it, just made you hope that you weren't fucking up a lizard's day or something. But it was unavoidable. The paths leading to these unexplored cliffs were never straightforward; in fact, there wasn't a path at all.

There was always some sketchiness, which usually occurred as we navigated different bands of rock, and there was a short vertical section on loose terrain. Somehow Tim and I always found these bands and ended up with some terrifying moments in between mellow hiking. Sections like this made us realize this is why the cliffs we were trying to get to hadn't been developed yet. For forty years, climbers had access to the low-hanging fruit of first ascents that lie oh so close to the highway with little effort to hike up—that era still continues in its own way; the main canyon of Indian Creek is far from climbed out, but entire walls to be discovered and developed lie at the ends of roads with healthy hikes.

In the middle of negotiating a sketchy band of rock, Tim and I saw the most peculiar thing—on a panel of rock, a basketball-sized object looked like it had crashed onto it. As we looked at it closer, the only way it appeared that something could have struck it was from the sky. We were amused, and we were amazed. I only wish we'd looked around more to perhaps find the meteor or whatever hit it, but sometimes when searching, you're only focused on the mysteries you're hoping to discover. And I don't know if I could find that piece of rock again anyway.

We continued up the loose cliffside and finally arrived at a wall. Relieved to be done with the hiking and excited to see what we could see, we immediately began our inspection. We walked the base of the wall with the necks of climbers, tilted back, looking above, always above. "This doesn't look too bad," one of us would say, but we weren't saying it enough. After an hour of exploring the wall, we'd come to the conclusion that we'd come across another bust. Maybe that's how the miners felt too, after they'd blown up a cliff band, hoping for uranium and only finding worthless sandstone. Cotton mouthed and sunburned, we planned our escape.

Anytime we'd have a bust, we'd call the wall Disappointment Cliffs Part Three, Part Four, Part Five, etc. Disappointment Cliffs was a long cliff band in the main canyon that stood right next to other fantastic walls, but it didn't yield many cracks, surely to the dismay of the pioneering climbers that hiked the walls and hoped to find what they had at most other walls in the main canyon. We'd been hiking a lot, but we never found much, other than the fun of exploring; the fun of exploring though ain't much fun unless you find something.

Still, there was another benefit—we found quietness and stillness. The art of doing nothing now had value, because it seems in society, with cell phone reception and all, we were always doing something. Not always something productive and engaging, but often just doing something that was essentially doing nothing. Once I had a smartphone in my pocket, it felt like a new era had begun, although I don't know if I really noticed it at the time. I was just amazed I had a computer that fit into my pocket. Shit, I remembered Mom and Dad's computers in the '80s and '90s; now that same accessibility was wallet sized. My buddy Dave called them hand brains.

And oh how they have changed our brains and our desires to be entertained and connected. What would Jack Kerouac have said about Facebook? What would Dr. Martin Luther King Jr. have tweeted?

Everything that was changing though also helped me become an independently published writer. As I steadily collected rejection letters for my books, I just published them myself and waited to see if people bought them and read them. They did. So I never lamented the changes to the publishing world that were brought forth by technology. Still, there was something about the constant possibility to go online, and I don't know if we'll be able to truly know how this affects our brains and society for some time. One thing I do know is that, even early on, it is hugely beneficial to disconnect from all of that and just be outside.

As the sun parched our bodies, we kept traversing this wall—maybe three or four hours into it—and the character of rock changed. Cracks, those cracks we've been obsessed with finding, started to appear. In vast numbers. At first, I wondered if they were a mirage, like water in the desert. Could it be?

I looked back at Tim, and he had that same stupid look on his face that I had. That validation of wanderlust, accompanied with the fatigue of the elements. *I think we found what we were trying to find*, I thought. I wasn't confident enough to say it; after all, I knew Tim would tell me the truth. Tim wouldn't bullshit me. When he started to talk, he was as excited as I was. I didn't know what we'd found, but I knew it was something, at least something enough to know that we would return, to rediscover.

Chapter 12

We had some unfinished business before we embarked on developing this new wall, way, way back in a forgotten corner of this land we call Indian Creek. There was another wall, the Dove Creek Wall, that we'd been developing in the main canyon.

One day while climbing the classic Annunaki at the Optimator Wall, I was glancing around across the canyon, trying to get the bigger picture, and a crack caught my eye. It was in the perfect light to be seen, and I rallied a crew of people, which included my younger brother, who was visiting at the time. My brother, Clint, lives in the New York City area and works as a lawyer in Manhattan. A dirtbag he is not. However, he is one of those human beings who seems to be able to engage and get along with just about anybody. On the drive into the canyon from Durango, he remarked, "This will be the longest I've ever gone without a shower: three days!"

I was more than happy to provide this opportunity for my bro and thought about our last adventure together. We'd gotten lost on a routine hike in Durango, climbing a popular twelve-thousand-something-foot peak, then promptly getting immersed in a thick fog, veering off the trail and then wandering down a drainage for six hours. Luckily, we emerged onto a highway seven hours after we separated from the group, and the story became our greatest adventure ever together, and not that time we got hypothermia. It was the most humbling outdoor experience I've had to date, and I was beyond proud of my brother for the mental tenacity and physical prowess he displayed during that epic.

That light, that crack, it shined so perfectly for that moment that it begged us to go check it out. Seeing a crack from afar usually means it's wide; you've got to see it close up to really know what's going on there. Indeed, the crack was wide up high for the finish, but the start was so thin you couldn't even fit a ruler in it. It was a beauty, and it had never been climbed.

There were other unclimbed cracks as well, and I vowed to return. Not long after my brother set his personal record for not showering, we began establishing this area.

The zone split a fracture in the interest of our crew—on busy weekends, we'd have up to twenty friends at a campsite—usually half of the folks were willing to do the necessary dirty work that a new wall demanded, and the other half wondered if we'd lost our minds. We wanted to do it right, so we were cleaning loose blocks, scrubbing the sand off with industrial brushes, doing trail work with heavy tools; basically the wall turned into a job site. This repelled some of our friends, especially the ones who'd driven hours and hours to get there and dreamed of climbing perfect splitter cracks.

Plus, this wall had quite an odd distinction: poison ivy grew in one section along the trail, the only place I've ever seen cultivate that evil weed in all of Indian Creek. My friend Shaun even started calling it the Poison Ivy Wall—he did not want this endeavor to catch on. Shaun is another one of my best friends, and I could write another book about our adventures together, but alas we obviously didn't share the stoke for this particular aspect of climbing.

Around this time, an old friend from the past, one who I honestly never thought I'd ever seen again, started coming back on the scene. Dane was one of my first climbing homies in Colorado. We worked together in various restaurants; we lived together and climbed together. We called him the Idea Man because he was always coming up with random business ideas that he never followed through on. He was one of my favorite people to climb with back in the day, but he got out of climbing for a long time, maybe ten years or so.

Amazingly, we just picked up where we left off—climbing is special like that, and equally as important, Dane was down with the Dove Creek Wall and all the work that needed to be done; he loved it.

What is hard to describe is Dane's sense of humor. I think he could have been some stream-of-consciousness stand-up comedian. Recently, when we were out at Indian Creek together, I decided to write down all his funny one-liners for a day.

Canadians are so nice—they all seem like they are serial killers.
It's nights like these I wish I had a V-Neck shirt.
Y'all got some of that Colorado wildflower? (Weed.)
Did you know that the taco has replaced the hot dog as America's #1 food?
That heel-toe is turning me on. (Said while I was climbing an off-width.)
Did you know that there's a rising rate of diabetes in raccoons?
Oh, man, I gotta see if I have energy in my getaway sticks. (His legs.)
If I had to take a Wu-Tang test, I'd fail miserably. (He loves Wu-Tang.)

And that's just one day! There's a certain art to enjoying the process with new routes, of being in the moment, and becoming one with the choss and the dirt, and Dane was ideal company for this.

So was Dave. Not the all-American mountain-guide Dave I wrote about earlier, but Climber Dave from Telluride, as they called him. Or Dimple Dave. Or 5.14 Gene. Or Nickname Dave.

If there was anyone who was down for the cause in Indian Creek, it was Dave. He embodied the essence of a stoked, positive climber. And he loved new routes. He had caught the FA bug in The Creek way before I ever had and thus was more knowledgeable about the ins and outs of new route development.

Despite the groans from my weekend Creek friends, the blue-collar experience of developing a wall was absolute paradise to me, even if the work was grueling and the challenges to remain safe were often overwhelming. The wall was located next to these giant forming arches, giving the zone a feeling of protection—perhaps the Ancestral Puebloans once stood here as well and gathered water—there was more moisture here than most places I'd been in The Creek (hence the poison ivy). *Okay, stop saying poison ivy, dude; no one is going to want to go there.* But, my point is not to entice but rather describe.

The first day of developing, we established two 5.10s right next to each other, and then immediately I desired to go look at the line that initially attracted me to the wall. Upon further inspection, I decided the line still looked prime, unique, and desirable—at the bottom, it was like a shrinking exclamation point—but there was a massive detached block some forty feet up, where it looked like the route eased up in difficulty. The block was about eight feet tall and four feet across. The cracks above, below, and to the side indicated a climber's worst fear, that this section was no longer a part of the wall; it was simply resting there unattached.

I wrestled, in my mind, with the possible outcome. I could climb up to this block, and I could pull if off, surely killing myself or the belayer, or both. Indeed, it would be worse to kill one's belayer with a loose block than to die oneself. The scenario tormented me—was this worth it? And did I have the willpower to walk away if I weighed the options and decided that the risk was not worth it?

When I was younger, I was led by the energy of a twentysomething. I did some stupid things, and I shouldn't be alive today because of it. Nowadays, I like to think I thoroughly analyze the situation before committing. This one was tough—I wanted it so badly, but was that wanting stronger than sound reasoning? In the end, I decided that I'd just go up there and see how it looked.

Since I'd just belayed Dave on one of the 5.10s we'd established, it was my turn on the sharp end. I carefully aided the beginning; it seemed impossible to free climb, yet the line between impossible and possible is very narrow, and if I was placing cams in the crack, surely somebody, if not me, could put their fingertips in there. I was worried about the big detached block above, not thinking about future free climbing efforts, and I was enjoying myself, venturing into a crack that had never seen the touch of human hands, with Dave, patiently belaying me and stoked on the moment.

I approached the block, and it was much bigger than me, probably weighed a ton. I do what climbers do; I banged against it with a hammer to see if it was hollow. A thud with zero resonation confirmed it was solid.

It was too big to fail was what I yelled down to Dave, and I 99.9 percent believed what I was saying. Soon enough, I'd jammed my hands and feet into it and mantled on top. It wasn't going anywhere, anytime soon, and thus it was destined to remain part of this new climb.

I climbed another twenty feet or so and then drilled two bolts as an anchor. The big question was answered: the block would stay, and soon we had a toprope set up to play around on for the rest of the day.

When a new climb goes up, there is the question of naming. Some believe a climb should not have a name until it has been free-climbed—after all, it is the free ascent that then establishes the climb as a route. I really enjoy naming climbs, and it's nice to have a reference to what you're talking about. I also believe a climb names itself in many ways, from a feature or a certain experience.

We'd named this area the Dove Creek Wall after a small, rural town in Western Colorado, right on the border of Utah, one of the few places for amenities as we drove from Durango to The Creek. The town is blue collar with a dose of redneck. The first thing you see when driving in is a Confederate flag displayed right outside a run-down trailer. The town was known for growing beans, and they called themselves the Pinto Bean Capital of the World.

In addition to their beans, we knew it for the Superette, a gas station slash supermarket slash fried-food restaurant. And at the Superette was an old lady who had a mustache, who, naturally, everyone knew of as the Mustache Lady. I can't remember exactly when I thought of it, perhaps on the drive back, but I knew this new climb would be called Superette Crack. The name also obviously referenced Super Crack, which was one of the first climbs done in Indian Creek and still to this day one of the most popular.

The Dove Creek Wall provided a mere seven routes, and we milked that experience for all it was worth. We returned again and again. I worked on free climbing Superette Crack, and Tim led the efforts to improve the trail. It felt like a sanctuary, a special place, like a child's fort or something. It felt special to have that space, with the expanse of Indian Creek to gaze across, knowing we'd leave behind an experience that others could enjoy. There's the greed and indulgence in new routes, but there's also a gift for future climbers that will bask in it in their own way—a win-win.

Around this time, since we were always armed with drills, we'd be sure to fix dangerous bolts when we came across them or someone told us about them. One time when we were on the South Six-Shooter, Dane pulled a bolt out with his bare hands. This sandstone was often bomber but the nuance of placing bolts was far from straightforward.

It seemed like this land's way of enforcing karma: one day, we would discover something new for ourselves, and the next day, we'd climb a route from the past that begged to be fixed. In doing so, we protected our fellow human beings from unnecessary risks such as a bolt pulling, which surely would end up in a major injury or loss of life.

The more I placed bolts, the more I learned how important the attention to detail was. The bolts that became sketchy were ones that had constant force applied to them, usually while toproping or, in the case of the South Six-Shooter bolt, while rappelling.

One day, a friend told us that she was climbing Annunaki the previous weekend and noticed one of the anchor bolts was loose. In fact, she was able to pull it out with her hand. Obviously, this freaked her out, and she didn't have a wrench so she simply tightened the bolt with her hand and hoped for the best.

After she told us this, we knew we had to rally over to Annunaki to drill a new bolt and remove the sketchy one. We weren't the only suitors of Annunaki—there were already five or six folks waiting in line to lead it—it's just one of those climbs that everyone "has" to do, and for good reason. The climb itself is worthy, a gently overhanging crack that formed the shape of a lightning bolt. The crack happens to be on this massive pillar that created one of the most special and inviting perches in all of Indian Creek—a large crew can hang out there and watch the show of whoever is on the climb. Match an überclassic climb with an epic hang, and you've got the stuff dreams are made of in the desert.

If these walls could talk, they would tell you they've seen some stupid shit. Suitors are often ill prepared—they often simply don't have the chops required to get on this rig. Perhaps the beauty stokes the ego, or perhaps it is that 5.12-grade that was once proposed. The scene at Annunaki often turns into this: competent climbers below have to endure an overstoker hanging from piece to piece unaware that they should have just opted for a lap on toprope to work on their skills.

Now I'm not saying that this technique isn't good for developing skills itself, but that is best left when there's no one else sitting around waiting in the queue—climbing etiquette is delicate though, and sometimes that pesky ego gets in the way.

When we were at Dove Creek, we could always hear what was going on at Annunaki; because of those massive forming arches and the bend in the canyon, there was a giant echo. They could hear us trundling rocks and shouting the nonsense that climbers shout when they are excited, and we could hear people cheering one another on for the send on Annunaki.

One day, we heard a couple of bros having a go at it.

"Arrrrgggggggghhh," one bro yelled across the canyon.

It sounded like normal climber banter and yelling. *Someone must be giving Annunaki a lead*, we thought.

"Duuuude, come on, man."

"Bro…do you even have me?"

We looked over, and the climber was a mere five feet off the ground, and already he was going into meltdown mode—a wobbler, as we call it.

"I'm totally juicing off this thing."

"What…the…fuuuuuck."

The bros were not doing well. This yelling reverberated so loudly we could hear exactly what they were saying. *Juicing off this thing?* we said to ourselves—what the fuck does that mean?

Well, as I thought about it further, you could call this *mansclimbing* kind of like *mansplaining*—bro language, something that guy probably invented on the fly as he got his ego checked when he juiced out of some perfect hand jams.

On this particular day, as we stepped up to Annunaki and hoped to fix the anchors, we were prepared for backlash—basically, we were asking to cut in line and climb it—but all thirty-seven people waiting in the queue saw the value in us fixing the anchors. Most modern climbers aren't trained in the craft of placing bolts and maintaining anchors, but almost everyone seems to "get it." In thirty minutes, we climbed it, removed the sketchy bolt, and replaced it with a new one.

I replaced it with a five-piece expansion bolt—later on, I'd learn that the glue-in bolts are the best for this type of situation; after all, the glue is stronger than the rock itself, and glue-in bolts can handle forces from a multitude of directions. For then though, we'd done our good deed for the day, and it was time to head back over to the Dove Creek Wall.

As the Dove Creek Wall shaped up, sending the Superette Crack became my singular goal. Eventually, after a year and a half, I'd tried this line more than any route I'd ever climbed before. Still, it wasn't coming together—I'd fall at the same spot over and over again, at an offset finger lock with no decent feet. First world problems for sure, but I was obsessed. I had to send this rig. My heart would simply not be content without it.

I'd drag anyone I could over there, and at this point, maybe twenty people had invested their time into my project. I was even making a short film with my buddy Greg, a young and serious filmmaker who I'd met in

Durango. Naturally, the Superette Crack made for perfect fodder for the film.

In the script of the film, which I wrote, I was trying to capture what the dirtbag life had meant to me, in the form of poetry. There had been a lot of essays and a couple films that had declared the dirtbag was dead—in the end, it was hard to argue; technology had changed the experience so much that it was almost unrecognizable to what it was even ten years ago. Smartphones and social media infiltrated—gone were the days of the lonesome climber, or at least the appearance of it. Sometimes I think loneliness feels worse now. When we're down and out in our lives, it's hard to look at Instagram—it looks like everyone is always having the time of their lives. But, that's just appearance—life never looks like an Instagram feed.

My poem was called *Last Thoughts on the Dirtbag*. It was in the lyrical style of Bob Dylan's *Last Thoughts on Woody Guthrie*—a poem about the search for soul and God in America. Here's a taste.

Looking for Something
I could not find trapped in walls
So I started searching
Started climbing walls

Then I was depressed
And dreaming of the sixties
Like something was missing
I wanted Jack Kerouac
I wanted to bring him back
And I wanted to just pack up a rucksack
And never ever-ever-ever-ever look back

One day, we were doing some filming on a Dean Potter climb called Salt Lake Special at the 4x4 Wall, and we met this character named Alan Carne. He just kind of came out of nowhere, and he was at the wall by himself. I love that about climbing—you never know what kind of character you'll get to meet on any given day.

Alan was British but lived in France. He name-dropped some climbers, and of, course, we had friends in common. He was wiry and short and overly enthused, which he had written all over him. He ended up camping with us that night, and the next day my partner for climbing bailed, so he agreed to climb with me while Greg filmed.

Meeting Alan at this time was godsent. He had been climbing for forty years, starting when he was fifteen on the gritstone cliffs of England. The son of a poor single mother, he would bike forty miles to these cliffs that lie above Manchester. He learned to tie a bowline knot from a local library and climbed on a sailing rope, using hip belays. When he really got into climbing, he was living on the doll, which provided about twenty dollars a week. He and his comrades would sleep in caves and all other sorts of strange places—even bathrooms if it came to it. "They were dark times," he told me. "The good ol' days weren't always that good."

Alan and I synced up perfectly. We talked about Kerouac, about dirtbagging, and the climbs we wanted to climb. At fifty-five, he was still climbing 5.13, and he was a more skilled crack climber than I was. When he belayed me on the Superette Crack, he watched me climb and then ever so gently offered me critique on my technique. I soon realized that the difference between success and failure was just a little bit of knowledge. Alan certainly had the intelligence part figured out in climbing; he was an athlete in his midfifties who was still at the top of his game.

It was a warm September day, and we were tired, but we wanted to get one last shot over on the most photographed climb in Indian Creek, Scarface. The climb is photographed so often for good reason: a splitter crack framed on an arête with the reservoir in the background and beyond that both of the Six-Shooters. Greg had just purchased a drone, and we sat in the parking lot waiting for everyone to clear out from the wall. Though we were new to drones, we knew it would be a dick move to use one for filming when others were at the wall.

Immediately after a brief test run, I was unsure of this drone. The sound was annoying, and it seemed invasive. Plus, having one hover over you as you're climbing seemed dangerous—what if the battery died and it came crashing down on you, or if it accidentally hit the wall and triggered a rockfall? Death by drone would certainly be a lame way to die.

Still, I'd seen drone footage, and there was no denying it was beautiful. I was just seeing how the sausage was made. So, with the last few rays of light, we tested out the drone.

Alan would lead, and Greg launched the drone off above him, the drone hovering and making its crazy buzzing noise. All day long, I'd been talking to Alan and learning about him and where he'd come from. In the middle of the drone-filming experience, while he was climbing Scarface, he yelled down to me, "Look at what climbing has come to. I used to climb in a Swami belt and a hip belay!"

There was no sense of malice in his words; he was just calling it how it was. In fact, I couldn't believe how generous this guy was. I'd just met him the day before, and now he was a character in our film.

In the end, the drone footage didn't turn out. Something wasn't right with the camera. And stylistically, I wasn't happy with it—a film called *Last Thoughts on the Dirtbag* shouldn't have had new, fancy drone footage. Greg crafted the work beautifully, and Alan's presence in the film was perfectical.

I went back to work on the Superette and implemented some of the nuances that Alan had suggested. They worked. The day I sent the climb I actually messed up the sequence but still managed to pull through the crux—some days luck is just on your side. I let out a huge scream that reverberated across the canyon—I was relieved. But I still hadn't finished the climb; there was a short off-width section that guarded the anchors, and I climbed conservatively and with trepidation, for fear I'd mess it up and have do it all over again. Although I'd just succeeded in climbing the hardest section of crack in my life, the important learning moment took place just after that—the lesson was to be in the moment and not to celebrate anything before it's all over.

I climbed that last remaining section and clipped into the anchors. The project was completed. I think to this day, it's still sitting there awaiting a second ascent. I think somebody could probably come along and onsight it eventually; that's how these things go—one person's project is another's warm-up. One thing I've learned in climbing though, at least for myself, is if I'm going to have competitive urges, it's best to be competitive with myself—to demand that I try my absolute hardest, give my best, be in the moment, and never give up until the send! Even if that doesn't come for another lifetime.

Chapter 13

*Standing there, gaping at this monstrous and inhuman spectacle of rock and cloud
and sky and space, I feel a ridiculous greed and possessiveness come over me.
I want to know it all, possess it all,
embrace the entire scene intimately, deeply, totally, as a man desires a beautiful woman.*
—Ed Abbey, *Desert Solitaire*

It was another dead end, but we shouldn't have been surprised. The desert had been too good to us these last few years, more first ascents than I could count—all types of sizes and lengths—we even established a line that went all the way to the rim. They were the types of days that make me believe in climbing; the golden age is always at hand. If not elsewhere, at least in the desert it is.

That day it was just Dave and me. If there was any partner I've ever had for the desert that I was equal to in terms of abilities, it was Dave—that's not a reason to choose a partner; it's just how it was. I would have climbed with Dave on just about anything if he were a much better climber than me or even if he only climbed 5.10. We just happened to check in at the same level. We'd work the same projects together, and often, one of us would send just before the other, or vice versa.

To write any more without describing Dave's stoke would be a mistake, because other than his sense of character—in my mind he defines what a climber is and what a climber should be—his stoke is what defines him. It's the reason we call him 5.14 Gene, not because he climbs 5.14, although I know he could someday if he wanted to, but because that was a Halloween costume one year. He has a 5.14 level of stoke, and if 5.15 were around when he got that nickname, he would have been called 5.15

Gene. His call, and our call, can be heard in the desert in the form of "Unnnhhhhhhhh."

Both Dave and I were far from stoked at this particular moment; this dream crack had dissipated into nothing, and we'd have to drill an anchor and rappel back down rather than taking this line all the way to the rim as we'd hoped. We'd been working on the climb for a couple days now. The first pitch, which we dubbed The Diva, was a forty-meter masterpiece—a few finger stacks but mostly thin hands for us, .75 and #1 Camalots. It was a dream and took virtually no cleaning.

For years, in Indian Creek, I'd embraced the communal nature of it, but the quiet days with just one or two partners, when we explored the forgotten corners, these were my absolute favorite days of all time. For the last couple years, there had been a lot of these days; in fact, my entire life was now planned around them.

The Diva crack was one of the finest. Five stars out of five, for sure. That day after establishing it, Dave free climbed the first pitch, in perfect style, and he sent me up on the second pitch. The second pitch was a fifty-or-so-foot chimney off-width. It wasn't terribly difficult, probably 5.10. I belayed Dave up with hopes that we'd have one more pitch at the top of the formation, and we'd have a rim route, a rarity in this day and age in the cragging mecca that is The Creek. Once Dave reached my perch, I climbed up and down and around and didn't find a crack that went to the top, just disappointing seams that didn't want to be climbed.

Disappointed, we had no other option than to place a bolted anchor and go back down. I got the power drill out of the small pack we'd carried along and began to drill a hole. I got about an inch in, and then it just stopped. Dead. The batteries had no more juice. We both probably yelled some expletives and then laughed at ourselves. How were we getting out of this one?

We should have also had a hand drill, but we didn't. We scoped around some more and confirmed the notion that there were no natural anchors, no trees or big boulders. There were a couple cracks we could leave some cams in, but if there's one thing a climber hates to do, it's to leave behind cams. It's not just the value; there's something about a climber's pride that we don't want to leave them behind unless someone's life is on the line.

And that was certainly not the case. We were alive and mostly happy. It was a stunning spring day, blue skies, red rocks, the usual in the desert—

beautiful but usual, no impending doom. I can't remember which one of us came up with the idea, but we ended up deciding to just downclimb the pitch. I rappelled down on a gear anchor and placed cams for Dave so that he could clip into them when he was downclimbing. I reached our original anchor and then put Dave on belay. I was thinking about how scary that probably was, heading down a brand-new off-width pitch in Indian Creek, sand and loose rock and all.

Dave's feet peered over the edge first and sent down some debris. I looked down slightly so the rocks would hit my helmet and not my face and then looked back up. "How you doing, brother?"

He was fine. He wormed his way down the crack, dust now covering him from head to toe, and removed the cams one by one as he went. He clipped back into our anchor, and then we rappelled down The Diva, back to this formation we were calling Beyoncé's Balcony.

Beyoncé's Balcony was this perch about thirty feet off the ground where The Diva began. It was twenty feet long and probably two feet wide and overlooked the Six-Shooters and the vast desert that leads into Canyonlands. It was a glorious place to be. Though it was only midafternoon, we cracked beers (we'd earned them) and sat around, basking in the awesomeness that is living in the moment in the desert.

We were calling this wall the Beyoncé Wall, thus The Diva and the Balcony, etc. Some day, I think there will be a study of how Americans named routes and how they corresponded with certain eras. In the beginning days of American climbing, the names seemed elegant, often just corresponding with the aspect the wall faces, take the Northeast Buttress of the Higher Cathedral in Yosemite. What a proper name.

But at some point, most likely when sport climbing came around, many routes had the most ridiculous names, like the types of phrases you'd hear in dick jokes and such. My point here is that male chauvinism dominated the climbing scene for quite a while and still does in many ways, especially amongst those bolting new routes. The other side of that is you don't have many walls or routes named after strong, independent women. And that's why we wanted a Beyoncé Wall.

In the process of our finds and developing these new walls, they started to catch on in popularity. It was all word of mouth, and almost entirely friends of friends, but at this point, after climbing in Indian Creek for nearly two decades, almost everyone was a friend of a friend. That's not completely true though, because Indian Creek was absolutely exploding in popularity, and so was climbing in general. Most started like I did back in the day—in a gym, and then they were unleashed into the wild by the hundreds. Every season, the place got more popular, and every season there were more climbers there.

My paranoia about the new walls being overcrowded was probably completely unfounded, that first ascent paranoia that some of us new routers suffer from. There was no denying I was greedy; I wanted all the first ascents I could get. Still, the reality is hundreds of climbers had already been to our "secret" wall, and 99.9 percent never put up any new routes.

Chapter 14

Once I sent my project at the Dove Creek Wall, my hunger only grew. Sure it was silly, this medium of climbing that had become my favorite form of climbing, not quite as silly as bouldering, but there is joy and genius in silly, in play. I just wanted to play more and explore more and find things that had never been done.

The kicker of this wall was that it was an almost-two-mile hike to the base, and of course, there was no trail. Dane got on board and showed that he was more than willing to do "the work"—plotting out a trail, trundling rocks, and brushing holds and cracks.

Tim was trained in building trails, and he carefully analyzed each and every step, not just thinking about this step, but ten, twenty, one hundred steps ahead. We'd seen many, many climber-created trails over the years, and we were determined to make ours a valiant effort.

There was one major problem to our trail—an hour into the hike, in a layer of Chinle, a decomposing band of almost purple-colored rock that felt like walking on ball bearings was what we began to refer to as the "death runnel."

The steepness and looseness of this runnel defied logic. It was just low angle enough to climb it but steep enough that whenever a rock was dislodged, it was sure to come pummeling down at a fast rate straight for whatever or whoever was below you. Climbing up the death runnel was always the crux of the day. We'd be an hour into our hike, sweating profusely, awash in the wonder of the red-rock world, half thinking this is awesome, half thinking this is stupid, and then we'd come across this damn thing. We always looked around to see if there was a better way, but we couldn't find anything safer or more stable, so we just went up the runnel. One time, Tim knocked a rock down on Dane, or Dane knocked a rock on Tim, I can't remember, but I do remember their thousand-mile stare afterward and us thinking that no one was ever going to come to our wall if they had to routinely hike up and down the runnel.

Once we arrived at the wall after an hour and a half of hiking, a certain sort of peace and joy would overcome us. The view, like many views in the desert, was like church. A view so glorious of mountains back in the distance, and canyon upon canyon upon canyon, one after another in Canyonlands, tucked into one another, a view that was beyond lifetimes of exploring, a view that contained past civilizations and eternal hope and at the same time despair, depending on how much food, water, and shelter one had.

After that settling, the prospectors in us came alive, and we sought out the cracks we wanted to climb. There were a few that were obvious gems: a crack that climbed in a cave and then exited the cave right toward heaven, a headwall crack that went for nearly a hundred feet, a dihedral that went for two hundred. It was as if we were old-school miners who had discovered gold.

We sought out what was the "low-hanging fruit" first. Mostly hand cracks or cracks so perfect from bottom to top that they simply had to be climbed then. We were so far from the highway we seldom saw any cars, mostly just those of jeepers, peepers, and hikers trying to access Canyonlands. We had discovered something, but we had escaped time, in our own way. But of course time is the ultimate motivator for the climber, because someday we'll run out of time and breath.

Having an eye for the desert as a climber is something that is cultivated over time, and really that third eye never stops getting more information, never stops learning. At first, it's the eye to know what size a crack is from the ground, and then it's the size the crack is when it's right in front of you, so you know what size piece to place on the first or second try. It's the eye to look at a section and know when to punch it until you get to that rest. After developing a few routes, I learned that that eye keeps you safe and alive; new cracks often contained something that would get you, be that a loose flake or block or a section where you simply couldn't get any good gear.

I had sixteen years of experience before we started the Cave Wall, but I still had so much to learn. One day, Tim, Dane, and I racked up for what we thought was some low-hanging fruit. It was a perfect right-facing dihedral, probably seventy-five feet tall, looked like a hand crack, and basically appeared to be like a walk in the park.

Soon enough, I was twenty feet up, leading, on the sharp end, and the crack was filled with sand and dirt. "This thing is an ol' dirty bastard," I yelled down to Dane and Tim, only to receive a mixture of support and heckling.

Not only was it dirty but the jams in the crack had a hollow sound to them, as if the wall wasn't fully attached. I plugged cams into the crack, and that made the hollowness even more apparent. It wasn't too scary, I was in a hand crack, but something was going on that I didn't fully comprehend.

I performed the ritual, reached the high point where the anchor would go, plugged some cams in, hauled up the drill bag, installed two bolts, and then began the worst part: cleaning.

Before I'd even reached the ground, I knew in my mind this thing would be known as the Ol' Dirty Bastard. As I rappelled, I used a toilet brush to scrub out the dirt in the cracks. Dust covered my entire face, and I asked for the boys to send up my ski goggles. I don't ski, but when I wear ski goggles, I'm usually in Indian Creek.

These flakes were the biggest issue. It's these moments where I always start to ponder time and rain and dirt and just how long all of this has been here. I start to feel more like a bug, or perhaps a lizard on the wall, rather than a climber, especially when we're the only climbers around for miles. And the more I tasted that, the more I liked it. I liked my company, my best of buddies, and even though what I was doing resembled manual labor more than rock climbing, I really reveled in the situation.

How many hundreds of storms passed water down the wall through this crack? How many lives of spiders and lizards did it take? Or do they just dig deeper in the crack where the rain doesn't go? And were the hollow sounds of the flake created by the constant flow of water?

Sometimes I wish I were a geologist, and when I'm around a geologist, I listen, but sometimes, out there, I just kinda make up my own answers upon reflection and observation, which is the start of science I guess. But I am human, and human beings just kinda make up things as they like, as they hope or wish things would be.

I started tapping on the flakes to see how easily they would come off the wall. If you're going to establish a cragging pitch with the knowledge that it will be repeated, it is your duty to ensure the person who comes along next won't encounter unnecessary death flakes and blocks. So we send them a tumbling down the scree field, to join in holy matrimony (forever-ever) with the other rocks in the talus below.

As I tap-tap-tapped on the flake, I asked Tim and Dane to clear themselves and the gear below. Chunks started to fall off with ease, and I realized what was going on was that there was a six-inch-thick layer of rock that was detached from the main wall but still remained barely tethered on. One tap with the hammer and a section would fall off, like putting together a puzzle but in reverse. I then regretted my decision to climb this thing that particular day but also realized I had a job to do. After a couple hours of labor, I called it a day, and decided the Ol' Dirty Bastard was clean enough. God made dirt, and dirt will bust your ass, the ODB once said.

Months later, after the climb had seen some traffic, I climbed it on a warm-up lap. As I was getting lowered, I gently bounced back into the wall and kicked off a five-pound chunk; with a bit of remorse, I realized I'd failed to thoroughly clean it as well as I should have. I found a hammer and spent another couple hours cleaning that bastard.

While I was cleaning, Dane and Tim patiently supported my requests, ranging from the hammer to the crowbar to asking that they turn up the tunes to keep my mind sane. They also dabbled in a potion we would only later learn was called purple haze.

Even though I felt like I was on the ODB forever, enough daylight still remained for another climb. And during this day, and every day the month before and for years after, more daylight meant another first ascent. We were still in the first month of this wall, and the low-hanging fruit surrounded us exponentially.

More important than the low-hanging fruit was that we had camaraderie in abundance. These guys were down for the cause, and with the spirit we had, we could have established a line on El Capitan. But instead of writing a novel or recording an album, we were just writing lines of poetry, sixteen bars of verse in the form of climbing lines.

Dane brought an intense dedication to the job, the craft. He was always there with enthusiasm to do what needed to be done. Tim was like a wise desert sage; after all, he'd lived amongst this desert for many years before moving to Durango and had an instinct of what the desert was and how to read it, as if it were another language, because it is. If one understands the language the desert is speaking, they can protect it to the best of one's abilities and capabilities. Tim knew where to put a rock on a trail and where to clean a rock off a climb, to put it a little more simplistically.

Because of the purple-haze concoction, their instincts and sensibilities for the sharp end were comprised, and lucky me, I'd get another lead in for the day. I'd learned from my mistake of thinking the ODB was low-hanging fruit, so I figured I'd go right for the best-looking line I could.

We stepped into the cave that Tim and I had stumbled upon the spring before on our exploration hike. The light was almost a purplish hue, not quite Prince purple, but a hue that was otherworldly and magical. Barely enough light shined in to see, but quickly our eyes adjusted to it. Once in a while, you get shown the light…

We called it a cave, but in reality, it was more of an enclave, a refuge from the world in the form of a broken pillar that leaned up against the wall and left a somewhat incomplete impression that one was protected while there. Not only was it a refuge but also we were most likely the first humans to use it as such, an incredible gift. After basking in those sorts of thoughts, I was given the sharp end.

Tim and Dane were awash in a couple different forms of purple haze, but still more than capable to belay and offer everything I'd need while I was venturing off into the unknown. A team of three can be really key for first ascents.

There was a monster refrigerator-sized block that guarded the perfect crack above. When I encounter one of these types of blocks on established routes, I approach it with caution but also the knowledge that it's probably wedged in there firmly because other human hands and feet have passed through. But when it's a mystery, there's much more doubt and fear.

The block was so large it would surely kill my belayer, but it was also so large it was probably there long before this land was even called the United States of America, maybe even before humans arrived to this land. As I climbed up to it with a delicate disposition, I confirmed in my mind that I trusted it. It's one thing to gamble with your own life, but to gamble with another person's life, well, that carries a little more weight. I was willing as I tapped on the block, listened to what message I thought it was carrying, pulled on it, jammed above it, and ultimately stood upon it. Fucking bomber.

It was off to the races from there, and I announced the size of the crack—perfect hands—to my comrades. They were stoked. And so was I. Nothing can go quicker on a first ascent than hand jams. I'd jammed my way up into a hand crack roof that led me to a chimney, and soon the left side of my body was wedged entirely in a crack, with wide hand jams on my right. Although from the ground the crack looked splitter forever, like most Indian Creek cracks, it promptly ended, or at least the high quality nature of the crack ended. Again, the routine of hauling up the bolt bag, sinking in a couple bomber bolts, and then the ever-daunting chore of cleaning. But, the purple light had left and was replaced by a dim glow; the cleaning would wait for another day.

Naming a climb is one of my favorite parts of the process of a new climb. Sometimes a name is in mind beforehand, but I typically find that name often doesn't stick, because you don't really know a climb before you climb it. Just as you don't know a potential lover before you go on a date. But this one was set before I even stepped to it—Purple Haze, all the way.

Purple Haze, I reckon, makes most people think of Jimi Hendrix and his famous song. We were inspired by that Colorado concoction and by Jimi. Later though, I'd learn that Hendrix wrote that song after a batch of LSD that Owsley "The Bear" Stanley concocted in the sixties. Owsley was one of those behind-the-scenes guys who was just as influential in the counterculture scene as Hendrix or Garcia. He was a financial backer of the Grateful Dead and helped pay for their infamous Wall of Sound system.

Though I didn't realize it at the time, here, with the Purple Haze, I could have stepped out of myself and witnessed this intersection. And perhaps I'm stretching too far, but going too far is what the desert is all about for me. Not just too far, but too deep, too long, go down some forgotten wash just to see what's there. To wander in nature with one's own humanity, stay out there so long so that the essence of contemplation is what matters. Be in the moment, and see something so you can savor and contemplate it later.

With the Purple Haze, or sometime around that day, I knew for sure that I was on the right path. I was born to be part of a counterculture, but more than that, I was born to be on the edge of two countercultures: both were dangerous, but if I could stay on the right side of both, it created a safe haven for me and my wandering ADD mind. If I'd been born in the days of The Dead, I really wonder if I would have gone on an LSD trip and never come back. I was simply too open to it but too sensitive to fully embrace it. Plus, those trips seem to have the answers in the moment but never in the aftermath. Climbing had something different; the aftermath always seemed the most holy. Like I'd gone to church and remerged anew from the baptism. But the desert had little water for baptism. It held a renewal as old as Moses.

Psychedelics opened doors to mental states I never knew were there, and I accessed some joy and mystery that I'll never really understand as long as I'm living. The space to explore is as vast as the desert. But psychedelics also gave me the worst awake nightmares, bad trips I thought I'd never be released from, terrible visions of a world gone wrong.

The best of trips left me in a trance, with thought after thought of high-level thinking, or so it seemed at the time. One time I walked around my neighborhood at night with a sock in my hand, just thinking, thinking—I wish I could have recorded all those thoughts, just to see. The worst vibrations though would destroy for me any hope that there was in psychedelics. One time, I set out alone, walking through my hometown, and the sidewalk started moving downward as I walked. A fire hydrant spoke to me. It was oh so sad, a downward spiral of vibration that I'm still not so sure why it all happened.

The use of psychedelics seems the most fitting at proper ceremonies with guides; though other than a cap, I don't have much interest in them anymore because of my bad trips.

I guess when I was cluelessly using them as a teenager, I should have had a guide. The insight and visions I gained have gone to the wind. But what little I do remember, I think that some parallels could be drawn between the psychedelic experience and the climbing experience, though that's a task for another mind. Doug Robinson wrote a whole book about it.

I can't say I'm anti-drug, but I know there're more bad drugs than good ones. I was bound to be attracted to that sphere, and some say climbing is a drug, and sometimes it feels like it. But if it is, it's the bubonic chronic, the good stuff, though it's certainly possible to have bad trips with climbing too. And sometimes, quietly and sweetly playing The Dead in the desert, I remember things, good things. And bad things. Death don't have no mercy in this land.

The Purple Haze route was a good thing, and in that beginning era when we were just starting the wall, we'd always have a long, strange trip ahead of us in the form of descent. Tim was envisioning a grand climber trail that was done in the best possible way for long-term use, meaning that it would still hold tough after rainstorms and windstorms and all the types of storms.

I'd finally partaken in the purple haze potion, and we all giggled and spaced out together in some grand communal gesture. We would place cairns where Tim suggested, made twists and turns where Tim though we should, and dug out steps where appropriate, always trying to minimize the busting of the crust, trying to make our path holy.

With these guys, that was as fun as anything else, wandering down in the dark for what seemed like forever, thinking we'd never emerge from the slope until we hit the wash, and we knew there were beers, chips, and supper in our very near future, and all was well again at the campfire, always and forever.

Chapter 15

We had half a dozen routes done by the time Dave made it up there for the first time. Of course, it was inevitable that Dave would be a part of this place—it was inconceivable to think of developing this wall without him. Plus, he had the knowledge, the skills, and the experience; he had that knowledge of the third eye for The Creek more than just about anyone I knew.

This headwall crack had dominated my thoughts ever since we began the development. I was sure Dave was game, even though it was late November and one of us was in for a long haul as a belayer. We reached the wall a sweaty mess after an hour and a half of hiking. I gave him a tour, pointed out the gems that we would embark on later, and then we got to work on our king line.

After laying out all the tools for the trade, confirming we had everything essential for the task at hand and didn't just so happen to forget something key, I started up a tiny splitter that accepted the smallest of cams. If I've climbed cracks that were smaller, I don't remember when— soon the crack ended and moved me rightward where the tiniest of seams awaited a decision. The cracks would never take gear that could possibly hold falls, so I drilled two bolts, one right after another, with that tense feeling, knowing my decision now would dictate every other ascent from now till eternity.

I talked it through with Dave, and I think we made the right decision. The wind was whipping, old man winter was saying hello, and Dave was probably freezing at the belay, but his trademark stoke and positivity kept us going. Plus a little Madonna; for some reason, she was on repeat on the iPod and gave us just the right amount of moral support. I'll never forget Dave sending up good vibes and singing along to "Like A Virgin"...*touched for the very first time.*

This crack was being touched for the first time too, and after some careful aiding, bolting, and cleaning of loose rocks, I stood right below the headwall crack. "What size is it?" Dave called out, and I announced that it was taking perfect .75 placements. After eighty feet or so of this size, I felt like I was leapfrogging cams, as one does on straightforward aid climbing on perfect cracks. I placed an anchor, and as I lowered off, we realized it was just shy of a forty-meter pitch, a perfect length for the Indian Creek megapitch of all time. Soon after, we named it The King.

We barely had enough time to get out of there with the last rays of daylight, the temps dipping to that bone-chilling status that lets one know the desert season is exiting and it's almost time for Creeksgiving. Dave and I were horrified by the death runnel, so this time, after a dozen trips up and down, we decided to scout around for another option for the trail. The chinle layer seemed to be telling us that this was never a wall that would have a good trail, at least not in its entirety. We wanted the full package though: quality routes, a good trail, something that will stand the test of time, work that another soul could appreciate down the road. Somehow snaking through the boulders and the cacti and the dirt was a section that didn't pose as many challenges as the death runnel did. So, in one day, we'd scored a king line and a better way to go for the trail. We couldn't wait to tell Tim and Dane.

Another Creeksgiving came and went. Partying hard, waking up cold and lonely and hungover in the morning. Loneliness that only lasts so long because all of your friends are there. It was getting to be a routine. But after that, it was nice to settle into winter in Durango and write. This year though, we started a new tradition of heading right back out the next weekend for one last session before winter really moved in.

We tromped up to the Cave Wall in the snow, falling all over the place, laughing at our obsession. We introduced our friend Adam to the wall, and he was quickly enamored. Adam was the little brother of the crew, younger than us, and also the guy who shows up to camp saying, "I forgot my stove/tent/food; do you mind if I borrow some things?"

Adam is also the best crack climber amongst us. And although hard cracks were his forte, sunsets seemed to be his favorite; he was always overstoking on the beauty, a good person to have around, always.

Dave put up his first route at the wall, the mega dihedral he named To The Moon, a single pitch that checked in no shorter than 185 feet. Dane and I established a more modest line we dubbed the Jigsaw Crack, a curving, jagged pitch that was pure fun.

And then winter's blanket was laid out, and The Desert became quiet again—it's a part of my memory that was always there in one way or another, but set in a forgotten wash of my brain for a little while, until spring awakened it.

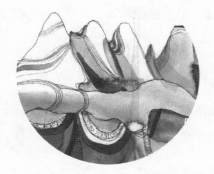

Chapter 16

That winter, I started corresponding with Annie, a poet and creative writer. Her words flowed as juice flows from fresh fruit. I started to fall in love with them, and then we started writing each other letters. I think we were both a bit lonely and got caught up in the excitement that is letter writing and communicating with another wordsmith.

I wanted to meet her, and one day I just came out and asked her if she wanted to meet in Joshua Tree; we'd both expressed our love for that place. I had a plane voucher stashed away for a rainy day, so in late February, I flew out and a woman whom I'd never met picked me up at the airport.

She was as beautiful as she was in her pictures and had a wild energy that seemed perfect for J-Tree. I'd lived there a decade before and hadn't been back since. It was the place where I'd fallen in love with desert living.

Our love affair was doomed from the beginning. It was like trying to climb The Nose in a day on El Capitan and you'd never ever climbed a big wall before. Things flowed for about a day, and then our ambitions and feelings didn't sync up. Time and space had failed to exist in my mind when I'd planned it all out back home in Colorado. All of a sudden, I was thrust into a place in my heart that this desert demanded I see.

Normally a good sleeper, I was spiraled into sleeplessness because of the carelessness of my heart and my words. I was a too-soon poet who had pursued another too-soon poet I'd never met in person before. Except Annie kept her cool more than I did. I was ready to start a relationship. When I expressed that to her, I immediately wished I could have taken those words back, as if they were a bottle I'd opened after already being way too drunk. But I was drunk on the possibility of love.

One morning, I woke up in my tent restless and heartbroken, or maybe just feeling the heartbreak of all those years. The sun wasn't even out yet, so I just replayed our conversation from the day before. Playing it cool was never my thing, but this was the worst. I wasn't sure where my heart was, but I felt it ache from head to toe. I waited until the sun came up and decided to embark on a solo routine that I'd had a decade before.

I watched an epic sunrise of orange, red, purple, and blue from the top of the Cyclops as I felt the place where my heart had been broken many times over. I said a prayer to myself, what it was I don't recall now, but it was a prayer to be in tune with my heart. I soaked it in and felt like I was a long way from home.

I scrambled up some other easy cracks—Joshua Tree is the best haven I've ever found for moderate climbs—and pondered the last decade of my life. I still wasn't where I wanted to be, but that me from ten years ago would have damn sure been satisfied that I was a writer. Maybe not so psyched on the fact that I was still rolling burritos for most of my money, but stoked on some sort of progression, moving slowly forward in the right direction.

Little of that mattered in the moment; I was heartbroken, embarrassed, and disappointed in myself.

I'd gone from so high to so low, so quickly. But, at this point, we were still getting along as friends, so I could crawl out of this shame spiral; plus, we'd agreed she would give me a ride back to Colorado, and then we'd finish the trip out in The Creek.

As friends, we got along beautifully; she was funny as fuck, and we had the same sense of humor. In some ways, we had so much in common it was astounding, probably too much in common to be lovers. We were just kindred spirits, and I confused that for the possibility of romantic love. She talked more openly about sex than any woman I'd ever met. She had so many stories, and time existed in a different sort of way once we took the flight of conversation. We wrote things together, simple things, but yet that was something I'd never done with another woman, or person. We had this connection—we could write together on the same page as one person.

I fiended for her love for the rest of the time we spent together that week, but she politely put up barriers; she did not feel the way I did, but did *I* really feel the way I did? Or had the lower chakra just been awakened by spring, and once that is opened in a man, do we just lose our minds to the will of sexual urges?

We drove for a day across the desert, back to Durango. She told me stories that were very personal, ones she hadn't yet written out for the world. I believed in her stories, and she believed in mine. We were a kind of soul mates, just not the ones destined to have a relationship, but I didn't come to that conclusion until months later—and I thank God or Whatever, because she was correct to feel that we weren't right for each other in her gut, and I'll always thank her for that. Because of what happened down the line.

Chapter 17

Connections. Connections. Annie somehow connected me with the greatest crack climbers that The Desert has ever seen. One day I was logging on to Facebook, and I saw a friend request pop up from Tom Randall. Now, I won't say Tom's a hero, because what's a hero, and can you call a climber a hero just because of what they climbed? Naw, but these people who push harder in climbing motivate me to push harder in my own way. I was excited—Tom Randall just sent little ol' me a friend request!

I accepted and then reached out to the guy—that's one of the beauties of this hyper-connected world. He said he couldn't remember but someone—Annie, I found out later—had suggested our mutual passion for desert first ascents might make us friends.

Just a few months later, I sat down with Tom and his partner in climb, Pete Whittaker, for an interview. Dane tagged along because they were his climbing heroes too. Most of us Americans had first heard of Tom and Pete, the Wide Boyz, because of their ambitious off-width tour through the Western United States in 2011 where they sent every damn notorious o-dub on the map and then established Century Crack. They later made a film about it—you gotta see it if you haven't already—and it has everything that's good about climbing films. There's so much I like about it, but something about the scene when Tom and Pete are challenged by Stevie Haston to go back to the Century Crack after they sent the climb with preplaced gear to do a "proper" lead of it, placing their own gear. They didn't have to, but they did, and they validated their ascent and set the bar high enough that no one seems to be following in their footsteps.

Tom had this line in the film that I'll paraphrase here, but it went something to the effect of, I like it when someone else doubts what I can do when I know I can.

I knew what he meant; it builds the fire. I don't get like that with climbing; after all, I know deep down in my heart I'm an average climber, my abilities are mediocre, and anything I've ever done that was "hard" was only due to persistence, not talent.

I do get like that with writing though. When I receive rejection or critique on something I know in my heart I'm right about, it's like jet fuel for the story—it almost propels it into being. We sat down with Tom and Pete in a room at the hostel in Moab, nothing fancy, and had a somewhat formal interview. Pete was more reserved and just seemed to want to go climbing. Both were more than friendly though, and I could have chatted with them for hours. At the end of the interview, I gave them some zines and a copy of *American Climber*. They went into Canyonlands, and Dane and I went to Indian Creek. The desert is big.

A couple days later, Tom sent me a message and said that he'd stayed up into the wee hours of the night reading my book. I couldn't have been prouder. And he offered some advice, well, maybe not advice but wisdom; all throughout the book, I lamented that I hadn't found the love of my life despite the fact that I knew love was all that mattered in the end, an ethos of the hopeless, hopeful romantic. He presented the reality that when one does meet the love of their life, certain freedoms that a climber enjoys are diminished. Again, I'm paraphrasing here because the messages are lost to the void that is the internet, but basically it seemed like he was telling me to take the ticket and enjoy the ride, you know, 'cause the grass is always greener. Thanks, Tom. You were right.

Later that season, I had the best single-pitch moment of my life. I write single pitch because it is my feeling that the best of climbs are the ones that stretch you the farthest into the sky; the multipitch and multiday climbs, sure, you have the lowest moments on those climbs, but the highest too, and you share it with someone, because the best things in life are always better when shared.

It was the shoulder season, when spring is turning to summer, and the crowds have moved on, but with the right weather, and a few clouds rolling in, there's this final possibility for perfection.

I am the worst at training for climbing. My body and mind know I should do it, but I simply rarely, if ever, do. I take comfort in knowing some of the best climbers in the world don't train either, but I also know I am an average climber and could benefit from training. Many times I wish I had the discipline that Tom and Pete do.

There's a natural sort of training that happens from obsession though, and I think it mimics some sophisticated training methods. I have read about training, even though I rarely apply it. Down to the basics though: there's a possibility to peak with every training cycle and season.

For three months, I threw myself at the cracks of Indian Creek, and now as the desert was greening, blooming, and warming, I was in tip-top shape, even if I wasn't fully aware of it. I guess love was on my mind more than fitness, and Annie happened to be back in the desert again. I'd convinced myself I was in love with her, and perhaps I was. My heart was aflutter when I was around her, and I wanted nothing more than to be with her in the desert.

The King made my heart aflutter too, and my experience on it intertwined with Annie. She'd belayed me on it a few months ago as our crazy "first date" trip drew to a close. It gave me a massive gobie—I even wrote a piece about that gobie.

I looked at my hand, the gobie that was once an open cut now nearly a completely healed wound. Of course, it was from Indian Creek, world-famous home of the gobie. Out there, it was a game changer—no more .75 finger stacks on the project. But, almost a week removed, I had a sort of sentimentality for it—the gobie was a physical reminder of two extremely peaceful days in the midst of a two-week climbing trip.

Annie says all my writing is about climbing and women, and everything circles back to that. I never really realized that until she said it, and then it was as clear as day—she was right as fuck. These last seventeen years that I've been a climber have not just been about those two things though—they have been a spiritual journey. Don't worry. I'm not going to get all Deepak Chopra on your ass; it's just the truth—the outdoors unlocked the keys to seeing my true self. And, I'm still looking into that mirror.

The journey toward meeting your true self is often described as an inner journey, and there's a lot of truth to it. But, in the world of climbing, you really can't do anything on your own. Every success is built within the community. Someone, Annie, had to nudge me back on that trail toward the real me.

That gobie: I know exactly where it came from, right at the top of my latest Indian Creek project. I was only on toprope, but I was making some horrific grunting, chuffer noises. Screaming—eaaaahhhhhh, uuuunnnhhhh, ahahhhhhhahhh—you know, those weird noises that come from Indian Creek that are kinda like sex noises, primal and reflecting a profound effort of the essence of climbing, that trying-hard thing. Trying hard is the best.

So I tried hard and screamed, and Annie was the only one to hear. We were in a remote part of Indian Creek, not rare, not that hard to get to, just an isolated spot where everything you do is work, so not many people go back there. Climbing becomes blue collar when you're putting up new routes in remote corners, but you're rewarded with a long-forgotten silence and solitude that most don't get in the modern Creek experience.

That gobie—it's so close to healed now, and it will be fully healed when I go back out to the Creek next weekend. It was annoying when it happened, but as the wound closes up, there's a memory in there I don't want to let go of—the memory of those two days with her, alone in the desert.

Like my heart, the gobie needs to heal; I think I'll put some salve on it now. Time marches forward, and we are all destined to be dust here in a few years. Everything good must end. Hanging on only provides pain.

Funny how distant those words seem now, as if they are someone else's, as if I didn't even live that. It wasn't even that long ago. In that situation with Annie, I had so much emotional baggage that I asked her to carry. But with The King, I have simple yet deep feelings, and that climb meant so much to me. Where was I?

Well, I'd just given it one burn earlier in the day, before the sun came around the bend, and with that exposure brought eighty-five-degree temperatures, pretty much ensuring that I wouldn't send the route that season if I didn't fire it that go. I didn't; I took a fall well below the crux, nearly a hundred feet into the route. Annie was belaying me. She was great, always sending up genuine stoke, and if she was faking it, well, I didn't care. But I knew she wasn't.

In my mind, very little else on God's green Earth than a spring day with cloud cover. The heat of the desert in late spring is defeating, my skin rarely burns, but my brain seems to, once I overheat, any optimal performance is gone.

So when that sun was coming around the bend, about to turn The King into a furnace, and the clouds rolled in, it was a second chance at redemption. We all went into the Cave by Purple Haze and cooled off, seven or so of us, ate cheese and crackers and cracked jokes. A couple hours later, I felt my pump wear off, and I knew I had one last go for the project, and then it would have to begin anew for the next season. I had limited time to use this fitness I'd built in Indian Creek—fitness that would practically be useless for my sport-climbing projects back home. So many types of fitness in this climbing world are only specific for certain areas. Indian Creek is singular. Part of me hates that because I feel like it's wasted time once sport-climbing season begins at home in the summer, but the other part of me appreciates its ephemeral quality. After all, climbing is this made-up thing that feels so special but is also, at the same time, so completely useless.

I had my ultimate best belayer in the pocket, Tim. As climbing partners, we're often on different levels. We joke that we're seasonal friends. In the winter, it's all about the ice for Tim, while I avoid cold situations as much as possible. In The Creek, Tim seems content all the time, while I'm only really content once I've trashed myself to the fullest on the cracks. Tim always sees the little things, the trail that needs a rock here or there, and he'll spend the time to make a small, minor thing that's wrong right. I always need to have the final goal, the big picture in my mind, always working toward it. But through our friendship over the years, I've learned more about caring for The Desert from him than anyone else. And, I've put my work in helping him with various trail projects. And we've replaced our fair share of anchors together too. You can thank Tim for those nice glue-in bolts on Scarface, an anchor that you used to be able to wiggle one of the bolts out with your hand. No one ever mentioned that in their Insta-Spraybook post, because no one ever noticed. Oh, the things we climbers trust our lives upon.

When I tie in and Tim's on the other end, I always know I'll have the best belay possible. It's more than that he just seems to be my good luck charm; I've sent many of my hardest first ascents with Tim as my belayer. Perhaps there's just so much trust and history between us, and it lives on through the rope.

So I tied in with that figure 8 knot of infinity, and I had that feeling of calm mixed with nerves—going into a battle with the crack, but in reality only with myself. It was the type of sport I was made for: competition with oneself.

The initial section of face climbing nearly spit me off—twenty feet up there's a thin mantle where you move your feet damn near your knees and reach up for a quarter-sized edge. The bolt below will keep you off the ground, but there's a scary possibility of a whipper. I mantled efficiently and then was standing up on that little edge, clipping the next bolt. The first of four cruxy sections had been navigated. After more face climbing, fifty feet up, I looked down to a string of six clipped bolts, with damn near ninety feet of finger and finger stacks jams ahead of me. The position was unique—I know not of another pitch in The Creek that The King can be compared to.

To try to give a move-by-move description would be impossible. The only thing I know is that I entered a state, *the* state of mind, that a crack climber wants to enter. First it's painful, and a little scary, then all of a sudden, all that matters is the try, the moment. The line is so fine between climbing and failing; you're right there, just trying, trying to hang on.

Soon enough, as I'd battled this crack with all my heart, I was clipping the anchors. Then, a feeling that I've maybe never felt before and likely won't ever again washed over me—"It was not me; it was not me," I said at the anchors. It was surreal, a complete transcendence that was pretty much the best feeling ever, perhaps because I felt my ego detach while at the same time realizing I'd climbed the most sustained crack I'd ever tried.

Chapter 18

We left for the summer. All climbers do. Sure, some folks might pop back in for a morning or evening pitch or two, but the desert goes back to the spiders, scorpions, snakes, lightning storms, and flash floods for the summertime. Summertime and the living ain't so easy there.

My summertime climbing escapades aren't near as interesting as the ones in the desert, just mostly clipping bolts and bouldering. Somehow, now The Desert would always remain in the recesses of my mind. That project I'd get to the next season, that crack we scoped that we needed to get anchors on, or sometimes just that meditation and the erasing of anything from the past or present. The ease of foot in sand or hands in cracks.

This summer was the summer Trump began his rise to the presidency, and there's some nausea that comes along with thinking of that—the reality that the civility of Obama was going to give way to a human who just wasn't my kinda guy, to put it lightly. But that's still down the road, and we didn't know what was going to happen just yet.

The creation of Bears Ears National Monument was something that seemed more inevitable in the summer of 2016. It seems like now it's one of those things that you're on one side or the other, because after all, I'm writing this book in the Trump years, and no one is getting along or in the spirit of compromise—at least, not on the internet. In my circle, there's no debate about Bears Ears; we all just assume it's for the best for climbers, and in my heart, I do believe that.

The present is getting in my way because I'm trying to write about 2016, those glory days that weren't really. Ignorance is bliss.

However, it seemed like this Bears Ears National Monument would be a good thing. Obama was getting his Teddy Roosevelt on: preserving an important environment using Roosevelt's Antiquities Act. His team was working with the Bears Ears Inter-Tribal Coalition, and when it was said and done, climbing ended up being included in the proclamation, the first time that had ever happened for a national monument.

Thinking of that time when we were moving from the Obama era to the Trump era feels like loss, reminds me that I probably failed in my vision of what College Me expected of me, and it reminds me of one of the greatest eras in my climbing life.

In America, so much is possible, and given my positioning in the world, I had reason to dream. The older I got though, the more I realized my impact would be small, but I could create change, and I could inspire. That was my mission, the reason why I was here. There was a sense of relief in my smallness, of the fleeting existence that we call life. I needed to see the fruits of my labor; climbing first ascents was perfect for that. So was writing books. But where was the fruit of my desire for lifelong companionship? I was reaching forty years old and had never had a relationship longer than four months. Freedom's just another word for nothing left to lose...

The day after I sent The King, I zipped up to Telluride for Mountainfilm for a book event, then zipped right back to The Creek. I was in love with Annie, and she was there. That night, I snuck her a poem before we went to bed in separate tents.

We climbed for a day there in The Creek and then made plans to meet up in Castle Valley. I'd wanted to climb all the towers there in a day, and Annie said she was down for a recon mission. She bailed at the last minute. I was already there and the text sent my heart into my stomach. She was heading back to California.

So with the parting image of the Castle Valley towers in my rearview, the spring was behind us and summer ahead. This is a book about The Desert, and for the summer, like most summers, I did not visit.

My unrequited crush finally came crashing down when Annie sent me a text late that summer that she'd started dating someone. I got mad at her for delivering the message in such a way. *Why couldn't you call and tell me that?* A shame spiral ensued.

I made up for those feelings with short flings with women I probably shouldn't have been with—harmless flings though—but it does amaze me how much the human spirit will look for something in someone they don't know that well. Oh, the heart wants what the heart wants, and so does the penis.

Summer used to be the ultimate when we were kids, but know I find the greatest joys in the spring and the fall. So, when Creek season rolled back around, there I was, back home in the desert.

It's crazy to think that this place that seemed like such a wasteland of sorts was being thought of at the highest levels of government. I won't bother glorifying Obama too much here; after all, he's a politician, but to me he *got it*—the people who wanted to see this land protected reached out, and they got what would later become Bears Ears National Monument.

In my years of plateau, I'd been ignorant of the gems that were here, but again, perhaps I just didn't have the right eyes, ears, or heart yet. There was a moment though, not long ago, where I feel like I got something, or at least felt something.

Dave and I had climbed some four hundred feet, repeating a first ascent that I'd helped establish a year prior, a climb that stitched together some perfect hand cracks with some other delicate cracks and pillars. It was probably as close as we'd ever come to painting a masterpiece, though in reality, it was all already there—we just dusted if off.

This climb took us to the top of a magnificent butte, a place so high and remote we wondered if we were the first people to stand there, to search around this island in the sky. The entirety of Indian Creek was below us as we marveled at our surroundings.

As I looked to the dirt, I noticed a piece of pottery—*could it be? It couldn't be.* I looked closer, black-and-white stripes. I looked around to find more and quickly did. This place that, moments ago, seemed so distant and foreign, this was a place where humans had stood a thousand years ago and broke pottery as an offering to the gods. A tingle went through my entire body as Dave and I realized what we were looking at.

Still, to this day, I haven't discovered the route that these Ancestral Puebloans took to reach this point. It was improbable and seemingly unreachable. It was the magic of The Desert.

Months later, while speaking to an elder Native American man, I told him about my experience, and he suggested next time I went back to leave an offering of some tobacco, for the spirits—something that would biodegrade. I told him I never touch the stuff anymore—what about cannabis? Sure, he said, that would be fine too.

After this particular climb, which I'm being vague about its location on purpose, I've come across more pottery and ruins. I never take anything and always take precautions to leave it as it was, marveling in a society that functioned here, in a harmony that it is at a higher level than we are existing at now. And most of all, even above protecting the climbing, that is why the Bears Ears National Monument is important.

I was traveling home to Colorado after the holiday season when I got the news. Obama had used the power of the Antiquities Act to create Bears Ears National Monument. That man had a way of putting my heart at ease, and he made me believe in the possibilities of America. We all knew what kind of storm was coming with Trump, and I felt like this moment when Obama protected this area would be the last of the things I would be happy about from the federal government for a while. It was a peaceful feeling, a victory for protecting sacred land, an agreement between the tribes and the recreationists. But it wouldn't last. Or would it?

Chapter 19

The day Trump got elected was one of the saddest days in my adult life. To put it simply: I hated him. I hated everything that he represented, and I hated that after such a thoughtful man was president, such an inconsiderate conman would be the leader of the free world. I was angry and sad and didn't know where to channel that anger just yet. All I had was hip-hop music. I knew Trump's election would change me, more than Obama's even. But I didn't yet know why or how. I just knew I was fired up and ready to fight for what I believed in.

A few weeks in, I got a friend request on Facebook from a familiar face, although it took me a minute to place it. I'd seen her around town, but mostly when she was in scrubs, obviously post-shift at some sort of medical facility, and I was in my work uniform at the restaurant, t-shirt, apron, and ball cap. Given that she was a beautiful woman, I didn't hesitate to send her a message, an almost knee-jerk reaction to receiving a ping. *How do we know each other?* I rhetorically asked. *And, maybe we should get together sometime for a cup of coffee.*

We went back and forth and agreed to meet up at the local coffee shop the next day. *I don't actually drink coffee* was one of the first things I think I said to Amber.

She did, but we both got tea anyway as we went through the motions of asking about one another's lives. We both thought the other was younger—turns out we were the same age, 38. She was the oldest of seven. We both disliked Trump. Dating in the modern age, you got to get these things clarified. She was a nurse who taught yoga. "I do yoga," I said. I love yoga. I do.

She did look younger than her years, a brown-skinned beauty, born to parents who got married young and, thank God, had her. There was a gray hair or two in her beautiful black hair, but I didn't notice. *I'm getting braces in a few days.* I was scheduled to become a full metal mouth for the next couple of years. I was embarrassed and imagined going out on dates with braces, getting spinach stuck in my teeth; it didn't seem like it would be very attractive. *Maybe I'd write a blog about dating with braces at 38,* I thought.

Our date went so well I wrote a too-soon poem, but in the wisdom of my years of expressing emotions too quickly, I kept it tucked away, for future sharing, if things went well. I called it *38*.

Chapter 20

Since I am a hopeless (hopeful) romantic climber type, my mind was always drawn to the anything-is-possible ethos. That belief led me to the best and worst moments of my life, the highs of climbing and the lows of unrequited love. It led me to falling in "love," and I put love in quotation marks because the more I learn about love, the more I question if I ever knew love. Climbing had guided most of my life philosophies in an unconscious way; I did believe anything was possible, that adventures can go all the way to the moon, and they can. But I was a hopeless romantic for sure, who had been fumbling along in my love life for many years. Climbing also teaches you to be persistent, which works for a rock, but not so much for a failing relationship; that said, I don't think anyone should ever, ever, forever-ever give up on finding love.

I always thought love stories had to be epic, and because I was a climber, mine would be epic. But, sometimes, love is just a cup of coffee or, in my case, a cup of tea away.

I managed not to exude my too-soon-poetry vibe too heavily with Amber. On our second date, I went to her Friday-night candlelight yoga class, and then we made dinner. Over beers, we played Scrabble, *two* games of it, in fact. Ah, the things one does on early dates, while you're waiting to decide if you feel some magic. The first word I used: LOVE. I shit you not. Not a lot of points, but a sign of things to come. And, yeah, there was magic.

Amber and I fell in love in the winter, usually the season where I'm not doing much except writing and getting out in short windows of sunshine. This winter had snow; they don't always these days in the Southwest. She told me she didn't really care to ski or snowboard much anymore in the winter and just liked to read and chill instead. I loved that a lot. We'd tromp around in the snow on runs; we both loved to run, but not too much, a healthy amount. We made pies and made love. And then we ate pie.

She was/is a nurse and went to Haiti to volunteer just a few weeks into our relationship. I admired that. Her heart was enormous, and she was the yin to my yang, or vice versa—I never remember. It was just perfect the way we got along; it didn't feel desperate or forced or just for reasons of sexual gratification.

She was in Haiti when Trump was sworn in. I went to the Women's March here in Durango and marched in a foot of snow. I missed her terribly for the couple of weeks she was gone, but when she returned, we picked up where we'd left off, like one does with a great book.

Of course, once things thawed out, we went to the desert. She had climbed years ago and still had her original chalk bag, climbing shoes, and harness that sat unused for fifteen years. She had even saved her chalk! I teased her about it—the chalk had lost some of its consistency and didn't seem like chalk but rather just a white powder that didn't seem to stick much to your hands. So, yeah, we climbed together, and later I'd try to keep up with her on mountain bike rides. It was a perfect combination.

I took her way out to this little campsite I like, way down a dirt road, far away from any people, and showed her this heart rock I'd placed on a tree the previous fall. She was obsessed with heart rocks and collected them enthusiastically. That's where I told her I loved her for the first time. She told me she loved me too.

Chapter 21

It didn't take long for Trump to come along and propose the shrinkage of Bears Ears; he even visited Utah for the occasion. The narrative that he delivered was that he was there to deliver the message that the time for federal government overreach was over. Yes, Obama wanted to tell the residents how their backyard public lands would be managed, and Trump was here to say, no, that's now how it's going to be anymore.

The real irony of all of this is that this is land that is sacred to several Native American tribes, and the conservation and preservation efforts were all made by working with the Bears Ears Inter-Tribal Coalition. And these were the original inhabitants of the land. If anything, it was their land being taken away—again—by overreach of the federal government.

I was grateful for Amber's love because the anger I felt was astronomical. I was thinking crazy and just might have done something crazy if it weren't for her. But was it so bad to be so angry? Or was it completely justified? Was I merely feeling a small percentage of the anger that the long-oppressed populations of "the land of the free and the home of the brave" had felt for centuries? I think I was.

With introspection on America, and seeds planted in my heart and mind to engage more in society, I think The Desert's meaning in my life evolved yet again. I still needed it, now more than ever.

The past is so complicated, yet the present moment in nature can be so distilling, so pure—that's why we go there to be in the moment—in a society that seems to be looking forward so quickly, into a screen. And so am I, and I so want to get away from it and be grounded, and the only way I can get away is to go where those screens won't work, where they aren't fueled by their almighty cell service and internet connection.

The Desert told Western America's story as well as I've ever heard it told. And it showed us what life is like and what it could be like. The land I love so much, that we call Indian Creek, had a heyday a thousand some years ago, and the original inhabitants, the Ancestral Puebloans, left remains and art that still tell a story. They had no written language, but the book can be read by exploring, with the right state of mind and heart. Their ancestors are still alive today as well, and they tell the stories too.

One day, in the early spring, when the daytime can confuse you into thinking it's spring in all its glory, and the nighttime convinces you it's winter, I finally got out of my usual routine, and Amber and I visited the actual Bears Ears area and hiked around some canyons with obvious ruins and artifacts from so long ago. As we climbed my truck up to a campsite below the Bears Ears sandstone formations, the view below was one of those views that made me think, *Yes, this land should be protected and preserved*, for the view even, not to mention the million other reasons, and the importance of this land to the many Native American Tribes.

That same trip, I was scheduled to give a presentation in Salt Lake City, up at the Alta Ski Resort. I told my story, what I know, the only story I really have—the story of climbing as a transformational vehicle, the kind of thing that saves lives, and if it doesn't save it, it will change it. I showed photos of my adventures in the desert, and I showed the short film I'd made out there. Afterward, the Q and A became all about Bears Ears, with audience members who were active advocates for the monument answering some of the questions I didn't know the answers to.

In the aftermath of Trump being elected, I, like so many other Americans, had to soul search, to wonder where we went from here. I posed that question to many who are more involved in civics than I am—from a state senator to the director of the Access Fund—and nearly everyone told me my greatest power was the power of the pen.

It's both humbling and sometimes frustrating—to write things that affect people's lives. It makes me feel small but important—not important with a capital I, but with a lowercase i. And it's important to know where one stands in life and what their role is in society. My role was minor, but it was a key in the music that is life.

On the way home, we needed exercise and craved a little more red-rock scenery. Amber had never seen Castle Valley up close, so we decided to take a little run-hike up there. I'd been there many times, and on the way up the trail, I had the thought that you never really know what will happen in the desert, particularly up there.

We hiked and ran and felt that feeling of the desert, which is much better than sitting in a car all day. A light breeze picked up. The sky was a familiar bright azure, the towers standing in a stark and obviously beautiful contrast.

We reached the high point for our day, the base of Castleton Tower, and stood there with the necks of climbers, bent, looking up at the small humans on a big tower.

On the hike down, carefully inching down on the "trail" of ball bearing–like steps, we noticed a climber lying down on the ground, surrounded by several other people.

"Do you need any help?" I instinctively asked.

Since Amber was a nurse, we went over to see how we could help. The guy had successfully climbed and rappelled the tower but then fell some thirty feet while scrambling down. He'd severely bitten his tongue, broken his ankle, and hit his back. Luckily, he was wearing a helmet, and it appeared that it would have been worse if he weren't wearing it. Several other people there had some wilderness-rescue training, and we left after briefly helping out. We were in t-shirts and shorts and started to get cold in the late-afternoon, very early spring air.

We heard a helicopter overhead. The winds seemed to get in the way of a landing as we watched it circle. As it did, I was reminded of some words from Ed Abbey, words that I'd read nearly twenty years ago, before all of these adventures: "When the traces of blood begin to mark your trail, you'll see something, maybe."

Chapter 22

So there we were, chasing that blood, that beauty, that quietness, and that adventure. Tim, Dane, and I had hiked for an hour and a half to arrive at this perch. There was a trail for part of it, but most of it was untrodden—exactly to my taste.

The sun was coming, quickly. It was mid-September, that time of year most of the crowds are still at bay; for good reason, the highs can hit the 90s, and that heat can zap any sort of inspiration, even if it's been building all summer.

It was our first trip out that season, on the shoulder of fall climbing season but still feeling like summer does in a lot of parts. The lead was mine; it was a dihedral I'd had on my mind for a while, one of those I just had to be the first to do, and if someone else was, I'd be jealous. I'm still gripped by the obsession; when it will release me, I don't know; I hope not for a long time. The hot sun was coming soon.

Our perch was plentiful but placed atop a forty-foot drop-off, a sublime place to be. Staring at the crack, I only saw one possible obstacle, a section where it looked like there was a detached block. It looked too big to fail, a statement I always 99 percent believe. We'd deal with that when we got to it; there was a large chimney where the belayer could be protected should I pull that block down while climbing through it.

I jammed and fought, quick bursts of movements in wide hand jams and then slower movements when the crack got bigger, jamming my hips and arms in. Progress was swift. At one point, Dane and Tim switched off the belay so that Dane could take photos. We've mostly been bad at documenting our first ascents, but since Dane was an aspiring photographer, we were going to start taking more pictures.

The view, that view, so always the same, the open desert with the Six-Shooter towers pointing up, leading to more and more and more desert. Desert forever. I'd never see most of it up close in this lifetime, but I'd see this view many more times. Up above me was a tower that had detached from the cliff; we were hoping this crack would allow us to access it, sort of a trick move, and the kind of trick that goes all the way back to the Lost Arrow Spire in Yosemite.

The crack was clean, clearly not a funnel for storms like many are. It was the goods, what we're looking for. There's almost always a challenge, a roadblock, and ours came in the form of this block. It was clearly detached. Probably weighed a few hundred pounds. Would I dislodge it with the 165 pounds of my body? My hands and feet would surely fit in the space between the block and the wall. *I've done this before*, I told myself.

In the climbing conversation one has with oneself, there must always be the consideration for your belayer, your brethren holding the rope is an essential part of the team.

I called down and asked Tim to retreat to the chimney, so if that block did come down, it wouldn't end his life. He agreed and started moving over.

Then, all I heard was Tim screaming. He had fallen. The rope came tight on the piece just above my head. I looked down to see Tim ten feet below where he was belaying me and a huge rock was on top of him.

"Help, help, help," he screamed.

All emotion shut off; primal instinct kicked in.

I was fine. I had a cam slightly above me so I didn't even feel the fall on the rope. I plugged another cam, and built a small anchor.

Tim could be internally bleeding; he could have damage to an organ or a broken bone. We might need to orchestrate a rescue plan right now.

Dane hustled carefully over to Tim and heroically lifted the boulder off of him. Tim is a certified first responder, but neither Dane nor myself are. Tim was up and moving. A good sign. He said he was okay. No broken bones, no major pain. No signs of a traumatic injury. His breathing was fine. He seemed to be okay.

He had taken what was essentially a simul-climbing fall, that one all trad climbers fear, and luckily he didn't pull me off the rock. The ledge that he was moving onto to get out of the way broke off, which sent him falling.

The cam slightly above me took the weight of the fall. While he fell, his hands came off the brake, but the GriGri caught me. A tragedy narrowly averted.

We checked with Tim again. He was indeed fine, nothing more than scrapes and cuts. This climb would be our last for the day, for sure, and we would slowly get out of there and back to camp.

But the climb wasn't yet done. I still had to get to a proper spot to drill an anchor. And so I kept climbing. An hour or so later, once I had an anchor, I rappelled down to that block that I'd eventually climbed through and over, and with a crowbar, I pried it off, sending it down, crashing a hundred feet past the ledge that Tim had almost fallen over, and it became another ledge a hundred feet down, with the choss and blocks below. I brushed the dirt off where the rock had been and rappelled back to the ground.

And then we packed up and began a slow hike down.

Chapter 23

When I think of the desert, writing about it, I think of the moments of leaving, which often can be a summit of sorts, emotions welling up and releasing. Usually it happens in the truck, alone.

A favorite song will be playing on the iPod, some Dylan or The Dead, maybe some Tribe. There is sweetness in that synthesis, and, in leaving, I remember why I came.

It doesn't happen every time. It's like fishing, a meditation in a sport of chances. But I know when the reset has occurred. I am momentarily free from society, from the knowledge that I am a part of this force that is only second to the force that is nature.

The truck rolls on, the magic of rubber on dirt roads. A slow exit, time to reflect, time to shed one tear or many.

The leaving, a climber cannot usually stay where we climb; we must move on. One cannot hold on to the sweetest of climbs or the deepest of anger. Leaving can be empty, but when I know I am leaving with something to go back to, the emotion is full of richness; and knowing this land, the desert, will be here for me is a comfort I need. To go on any further without wild land seems impossible, like going on without love.

I have both, and in the end, what else can a man ask for?

Some tears, yeah, some tears. Breaking through when they realize no one else is around to see them. Why they need to come out like this I don't know—it's just how it is? Maybe it's because I'm an American man. I'm just glad they decided to arrive.

They fall, and with their falling—in that moment—anger is stalled, and appreciation for the moment and the fortunes of fate float to the top.

Usually I leave the desert in a moment of too much wind, too much heat, or too much desert. Those moments are part of it—too much love, too much beauty, but exactly what I want and need and not any more, or any less, that's when the desert is my home, if only for the moment, of course, when I'm leaving.

Leaving always leads to coming back. I've contemplated the idea of moving closer to this desert, but I've realized my home in Durango on the edge of the mountains and the desert is just as important as my trips to the desert. The small things in life, like a hot shower and a comfortable bed, seem so luxurious after roughing it in the desert. The more dirt that washes off my body after a trip to the desert, the better it probably was.

With each return, I know the place can change. Areas that were once virgin, where we completed first ascents that are now published in guidebooks, can seem completely different. It often depends on the company; some climbers these days seem to be driven by a force I cannot understand. When climbing is simply all about just climbing, and a climber only cares about what they climb and their ego, something is lost. There's an art to our sport, but I guess it takes some time to cultivate that third eye for it.

Here I go, *kids these days*. I'm turning forty just as I turn this book in for publication. It's not the age though; actually, some younger climbers are on the same wavelength that I am. But my wavelength has been all over the place over the years; I've stood high and proud on a mountaintop, but I've also been drunk in camp, loudmouthed, egotistical, and incoherent.

In all honesty, I'm just trying to get back to a place, a place I felt so long ago. Trying to get back to a quietness, trying to remember exactly why climbing became so important to me. Nearly every profound memory in climbing was shared with only one or two other people. It was away from the roar of the crowd; the noises were those of the river, the birds, the wind, and the trees. There was an unequivocal feeling of meditation and oneness. A feeling like everything was going to be all right. A knowingness that nature would provide the highest of highs—we could put the drugs away.

For some reason, I try to find this in the desert. The desert is big; there's always a place to find silence. And the more time you waste wandering in the desert, the more you know. Worlds open up. Things can be seen.

Is it the spirits? Is it the American spirit to keep reinventing, to keep discovering? Is it that human nature to keep going after that thing that made you feel the best ever, to have the best days ever?

For now, it's hope. It's the hope that the president isn't giving me, society rarely delivers it, and I've got no set of beliefs that ensures everything is going to work out in the end.

So, I'm either punch-drunk or a hopeless romantic, coming back for more. But I believe in believing in something. I believe in following hopes and dreams, and I believe in love. I know from those searches, those whims, that sometimes, at the right time, they lead to the most beautiful things.

The End.

Last Thoughts on the Dirtbag

You know for me it all began looking
Looking for something real in this world

In the nineties
At the time "keep it real" was the phrase
We are talking like "back in the days"

Looking for Something
I could not find trapped in walls
So I started searching
Started climbing walls

Then I was depressed
And dreaming of the sixties
Like something was missing
I wanted Jack Kerouac
I wanted to bring him back
And I wanted to just pack up a rucksack
And never ever-ever-ever-ever look back

And something was missing
And Kerouac was long dead
And so were the Grateful Dead

But it wasn't time related
really everything is related
And the only time we have is now

So I picked up a pen
Nothing,
again and again
Like always before
Cuz I had no story to tell
Yet
No story to sell yet
So I picked up a pipe
And I picked up smoking
And I started choking
Something was missing

In the midst of all the dope
I picked up a rope
I picked up some hope
Because my friends
It's either have heroes or have heroin

And the sharp end
Is better than the needle
But we all just want to feel

But
The rope was dangerous
And hope was dangerous

But it's good to be dope
And even to live a life
Even to be born
Into this world
Is dangerous

So here we are
And there we were

Doing it for the glory
Naw
Doing it for the story
Naw
Doing it for the poetry
Yeah

We were just two dope boyz
In a Cadillac,
Ha.
Rather that
We were two dope boyz
In a Subaru hatchback
Way before hashtags
When we didn't even know we were dirtbags
It was good to be a dirtbag

It was good to see
Sea to shining sea
Good to see America
Is not all just all malls, cars, prisons, churches, and bars

Good to see there's some heroes left
Because all the heroes went left
Because you know it all started after I left
My past behind
So I could rewrite my future
Still no matter where you go
You are what you are
Player

And I'm just a rhyme sayer

I wanted to write
I wanted to sink
Into the paper
Like I was ink
When I'm climbing I'm trapped within the climb
I escape when I finish the line

I wanted to write something inspired by the sky, the rocks
Like you know forgetting about grades and clocks
And finding men and women who climb rocks

With all respects to the homey Jay-Z
I gotta tell you the truth B
It was not an empire state of mind
Then
I was in a dirtbag state of mind

You know because I learned
I could dig poetry
I could dig rappin'
I could dig scrappin'

I could dig jammin'
Hands, fingers, and feet
Whatever it took to make ends meet

Every day begun
With the sun
And retired
With the fire

Looking for hope over every bend
Hoping each and every day would never end
Never ending feeling of climbing, so Zen
So Zen, we had to do it, again and again

It took us everywhere,
From J-Tree to Yosemite
From Devil's Lake To Devils Tower
Smith Rocks to random rocks
We forgot about

But it always took us back to this desert
of
Red Rocks
No clocks
Blue sky

No lie
Only the truth of pain, grits, and guts
Showing themselves in pride, and cuts
Red dirt on everything you own
Red dirt in everything you own

No suit and tie shit
Just climbing it

And forgetting what you looked like
Forgetting that this world just ain't right

Ed Abbey
He was gone too,
But in our hearts,
Desert Solitaire was like dessert
For the soul
The desert is for the soul

The Colorado Plateau
Like Rock 'n' Roll
Like Hip-Hop
We wouldn't stop
Oh hell no

We soon found we were carriers of a torch
Those who are too mad
Too beat, to be sad
All the time
All the rhymes
Wrote themselves

Living in poetry
Living like this life was meant to be
My friends
Because it is

It's about that hope you have
And that feeling like dope you have
So where do you look for this hope that you're seeking?
Where do find that campfire that's a burnin'
That will light your life for the rest of its days?

You can either look to the church of your choice
Or you can look for Bob Dylan in his golden days
Either way you'll find them both in Indian Creek at sundown

Go To The Desert

Go to the desert
Or whatever place
Is The Desert
To You
For me it's The Desert
You know why I capitalized that shit

The blue sky
Doesn't know that Donald Trump is president
And maybe, you too
Should forget about that just, just for a second
Breathe.

It's not your fault the world has gone cray
That's not a typo; the world is cray cray

It's not your fault Donald Trump is president
He is an accurate reflection of direction
Where people are going
What they are going to be

But that's not you and me, babe

We gotta find another way
Gotta live for a better day

So you and me
We'll
Go to the desert
'Cause the sky does
Not know Donald Trump is president

As Royal Robbins looks down upon us
And knows why
We
Go to the desert.

Blue Eyes Climbing in the Rain

In the desert it rains
In the desert climber brains
Can think of nothing but climbing
But climbing is not the answer
Climbing after a good rainstorm
Was the result of a bad brainstorm
Instagram has your mind warped
Get back to your conscious
Your common sense
Don't take this sandstone for granite
It's as delicate as a flower
And your power
You rock climber
Is magnificent
I know you, Supercrack climber
Love climbing
I love you, Indian Creek climber
And I love climbing too
But do you love it more
Than a broken hold
And broken bones
From pulled gear
Climbing after the rain
Comes from a place of fear
Or stupidity, I don't get it

Actually I do
I want to climb too
Climbing in the desert is more art, than sport
Philosophically, and intrinsically
We will get more out of it,
If we listen to nature and wait
This is a planet out of balance
But on the rock we find our balance
But why rush that?
Here's a simple equation
It's the opposite of copulation
Dry is good
Wet is no-gud (like the Banditos)
After every rainstorm
Take a good brainstorm
Or a rest day

Even if you don't need
A rest day
Make it your best day
Drink some coffee
Drink some tea
Drink a beer
Smoke 'em if you got 'em
Yoga could be the answer
Make love in a tent
Or a long hike up a forgotten wash
Milt's burgers are the bomb
And food trucks are all over in Moab
Find the wild turkeys
Or petroglyphs
Light a spliff
Look at flowers
Or trees, birds, please
This desert is full of wonder
And climbing is just another
Thing we do
It can't be all we do
Wait a day
Build the fire
For sending
In ending
Just please trust me
And old D (for dirtbag)
Climbing in the desert
After the rain
Ain't good for nobody's brain.

Just a Climber (for Bears Ears)

At 40 I always thought
I would write something
I thought I would incite something
I thought I would enlighten someone,
something, anything
But here I am
In Indian Creek
Bears Ears
Just a writer
Just a climber
They say you gotta pick your battles
Now I know
Mine is finally here

Because
Without this here
I am...
Just a dot on a rock
That can't get all my rocks off
On the dot com

'Cause, here, and only here
I belong
Here, and only here
I see the way.
I see sea to shining sea
In this land that used to be the sea
Here, I see Me.
I see a world moving along at the speed of need and greed
And when we're out here we move along at the speed of need

This land is the only way I'm thinking this way
The only reason I'm not heavily drinking today
Or in some jail cell, in some place so far away

But this is today
And millions are in a cell
And millions are addicted to their cell
But that Twitter shit
Won't work here

So the importance
The importance of this
This omnipotent-ness

This bliss

She knows, she knows
Mother Nature
I'm writing her poetry
In my own language
Not the first that she has heard
This land is not my land
This land is our land
Now.

They call it the Antiquities Act
You know Teddy Roosevelt
The racist land protector
The false hero
Like so many American presidents

But left a good idea behind
While society climbed
Toward better ideals

Is it better to be idealistic
Than to be so specific

That all this land is to conquer
Because what if
We want to prosper

What if we still want to encourage thinking
Not the drinking of this orange-faced Kool-Aid

Drop it if you think is political.
This about the right thing.

This is moral.
Operating between two worlds
This, America

Being all
Seeing all
Stealing all.

And this idea.
Public lands.
Land for recreation.
Land for re-creation

Land to pray to
Land to be a witness to.

Land which I could never describe
Not with a million words.

But I'm not a writer
Or even a climber
Or writing this
Or climbing this

This is
America

My America, Your America, Our America

Let's pick the battle
And win the fight

About the Author

Luke Mehall lives in Durango, Colorado. He is the publisher of *The Climbing Zine*, an independent print publication and website, and he is the author of *American Climber*, *Graduating From College Me*, *The Great American Dirtbags*, and *Climbing Out of Bed*. He enjoys climbing, sleeping in tents, hip-hop, yoga, vinyl, typewriters, Scrabble, and uninterrupted mornings of writing. In 2017, his mustache was named the best of Indian Creek.